Table of Contents

Acknowledgements

*The material on which this book is based has been collected over a period of
some twenty years, during which I have been greatly assisted by many people who
have kindly lent me items from their personal archives or have told me of memories
about the town that have been passed down to them by their forebears.
Many thanks are due to the Bassetlaw Museum for providing photographs, illustrations and advice.*

The Book of Retford

by
James Roffey

Bookworm of Retford

Published by
Bookworm of Retford
Spa Lane, Retford, Notts. DN22 7PB

ISBN 095516740X

First published 1991 by Barracuda Books Limited
This edition 2005 by Bookworm of Retford

Printed and bound by
Burgess Photo Print Ltd.
Beehive Street, Retford

Introduction

RETFORD, ANCIENT MARKET TOWN, say the huge signs beside the A1 trunk road as it sweeps through Nottinghamshire. On other, less busy roads there are further signs, but these are more discreet and bear the words BOROUGH OF EAST RETFORD - FIRST CHARTER 1246, thereby giving a hint of the long history of which the town is so justifiably proud.

Travellers to Retford should be forgiven if they sometimes become confused because, at first glance, in the place name index of many road guides, the town does not appear to be mentioned. There are really two Retfords and you must look under E for East Retford and W for West Retford.

However, as far as the post office, railways and the road signs departments of the various transport authorities are concerned, the name is simply RETFORD.

Originally there was only one Retford and that was a tiny village on the western bank of the river Idle but, when a settlement sprang up on the eastern bank, it became necessary to distinguish between the two. We then had East and West Retford as two separate places, each with its own parish church and self-governing as far as local matters were concerned. Of the two it was East Retford that prospered and developed into a corporate borough and thriving market town.

When the boundaries of the Borough of East Retford were extended during the 1800s to incorporate its smaller neighbour, it would perhaps have made sense to drop the east and west prefixes and simply call it the Borough of Retford, but that was not to be. Perhaps in those days civic pride and a strong sense of tradition prevented such acts of rationalisation.

The story of Retford contains many anomalies; indeed it is remarkable that in view of its early disadvantages the place ever developed into a thriving market town. The fact that it did, indicates a spirit of determination, resourcefulness and independence for which the town is still noted.

This book attempts to tell that story and to trace the growth of this remarkable market town.

This is how it once was — Holoran & Co of Retford produced this postcard view of 'The River Idle at Retford' early this century — the ink factory building on the right is still there.

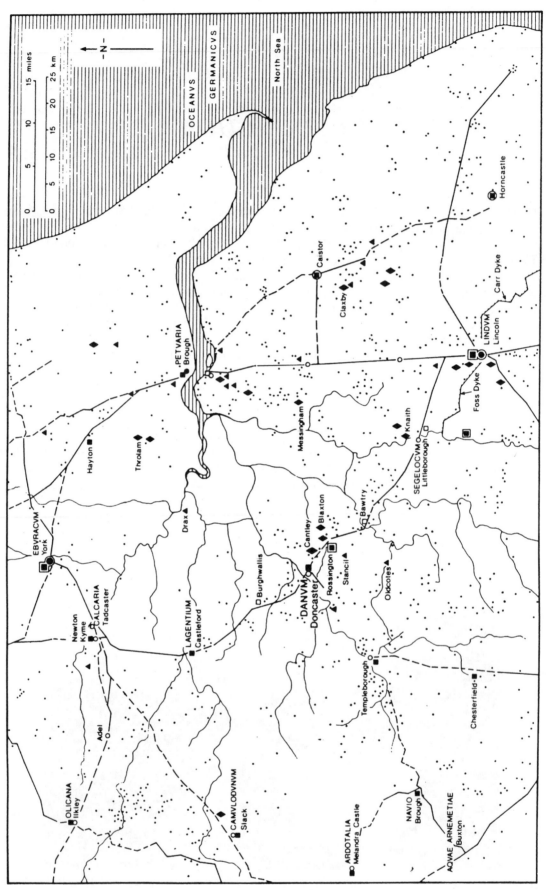

Roman roads and sites.

Before the Charters

HOW ancient is the market town of Retford? That is a question to which historians have so far failed to provide an answer, because little is known about it before the first of a series of charters was granted. Some writers have suggested that East Retford, in common with Bawtry, was one of several new towns created in the 12th century, but the absence of a road layout on the grid system makes that improbable.

It was also thought that the Roman period bypassed the area, but that was disproved when fragments of Roman pottery were found when the river Idle was dredged in 1898. Aerial photographs also indicate field boundaries believed to be those of Romano/British farms. The boundary marks continue towards the town right up to the present built-up area, so that some of today's houses must stand on land that grew crops for Roman soldiers.

Somewhere in Retford is the site of a Roman farmhouse, perhaps more than one. But where they stood or how their broken pottery came to be in the river Idle is something we may never know.

The nearest Roman settlement of any importance was nearly ten miles to the east at the place we know as Littleborough, then called Segelocum. This was where the Romans had constructed a paved ford across the river Trent on the route of their road from Bawtry to Lincoln. Parts of that road still exist and are in use to this day, the village of Clayworth lies alongside it, and its route can easily be traced on a map.

In Roman times Littleborough was much larger and an important staging post, where footsore soldiers could rest overnight before continuing their march. Possibly crops grown on the site of Retford were carried here to Roman kitchens. Littleborough was important because of its river crossing; the ford continued to be used long after the Romans departed. It may have been one of the reasons why East Retford became a market town.

After the Roman period, with its carefully maintained roads, heated buildings and well ordered farms, north Nottinghamshire entered a turbulent time. First came the Saxons to establish the kingdom of Mercia. They created villages and built many churches, but not, it seems at Retford, where neither of the two parish churches has Saxon origins. Trouble for the Saxons began when the Vikings started to raid their villages, carrying off everything of value and burning the thatched buildings as they left.

Using the incoming tide, the Viking raiders, mostly from Denmark, would sail up the rivers in their longboats, penetrating far inland to wreak havoc and destruction. Although they were obviously a great nuisance to the Saxons and feared by the virtually defenceless villagers unfortunate enough to live within striking distance of coast or rivers, the early Vikings did not pose a serious threat to the authority of the Saxon kings. But as the years went by, so the time spent in England by the raiders began to lengthen until, in the year 864, they decided to stay during the winter months rather than face the voyage across the sea.

This resulted in the establishment of Danish settlements and soon they were to depose the Saxon kings of Mercia, Northumbria and East Anglia and take over their lands. Nottinghamshire came completely under their rule and was part of what is known as the Danelaw.

The Danes put their own names to their settlements, and many Danish place names ended with the suffix *by*, such as Ranby, Barnby, Saundby and Scrooby. Other evidence of Danish influence can be found at Clayworth with its Toft Dyke Lane, which means the house (toft) with a lane beside a dyke.

Naturally, the Saxon kings resented losing their lands and one of them, Athelstan, marched north to regain control. Instead of fleeing, the Danish settlers stayed, accepting him as king. But not long after, one of the fiercest Vikings, Sven, sailed from Denmark and conquered York, driving the Saxon king Ethelred, who had succeeded the able Athelstan, into exile.

A year later Sven died and was succeeded by Cnut, king of Denmark. During his absence to establish his rule there, Ethelred returned to England, raised an army, marched north to Gainsborough, and forced the Danes to take ships and depart. It was all in vain, for Cnut returned.

Already the dozens of small villages that were to look upon Retford as their market town were becoming established. One name, that of *Bassetlaw*, was in use during Saxon and Viking times to denote an administrative area. To the Saxons our part of Nottinghamshire was known as the Hundred of Bassetlaw, to the Danes it was the Wapentake of Bassetlaw. Many years later the name was given to a parliamentary constituency and to a district of local government.

Over many years, power vacillated between Saxons and Danes, until eventually England was united under a Saxon monarchy. Church building flourished as the country settled to a period of peace and several examples of Saxon architecture survive in north Nottinghamshire. In 1066 that peace was shattered.

William the Conqueror awarded much of the old Saxon kingdom of Mercia to one of his closest supporters, Roger de Busli. He built a castle at Tickhill and set about the systematic subjection of the area. The Norman survey of England known as the Domesday Book, carried out in 1086, included a reference to Retford — *Redforde: Archbishop of York; Roger de Bully. Mill.* It is generally believed that the reference was to what we know as West Retford and that either East Retford did not exist or it may have been the place referred to as *Odestorp*. The mill would have been a water mill on the river Idle, probably at Bridgegate.

The Normans were great church builders and many churches in the Retford area were built or enlarged then. Examples of Norman arches, porches, etc. are still quite numerous but their tiny church at Littleborough is a gem. It is one of the smallest in England and its charm lies in its simplicity.

During the years of comparative stability which followed the Norman takeover, north Nottinghamshire's villages expanded but much of the countryside was still undeveloped. The trees and ferns of Sherwood Forest covered a much larger area than now, and extended virtually to the western outskirts of Retford. Between West Retford and Blyth lay the wild area of Barnby Moor and to the south Markham Moor was equally inhospitable and dangerous to travellers.

Most of West Retford stood on a slight hill beyond the reach of flooding from the river Idle, but its lower levels were usually waterlogged. The land on which East Retford was later developed was particularly vulnerable to flooding; it was both marshy and unstable, which was to cause problems for many builders. Some failed to get it right and the result can still be seen in the Market Place, where at least one building has a noticeable sag.

The river Idle is made up of the waters from three rivers — the Maun, Poulter and Meden. It is joined by the river Ryton and between them they drain a vast area, reaching into Derbyshire and South Yorkshire. In times of heavy rain the volume of water flowing in the Idle increases dramatically and the name of the river becomes somewhat inappropriate. All of this water is now discharged into the river Trent but, prior to the vast drainage scheme at Hatfield Chase and the Isle of Axholme, (instigated by Charles I) the Idle was connected to the river Don, which it reached *via* a tortuous and sluggish channel.

A Roman fortlet at Scaftworth, near the old Roman road between Bawtry and Clayworth.

Sir Cornelius Vermuyden, the Dutch drainage expert who carried out the King's works, diverted the river to meet the Trent at West Stockwith and that greatly improved the conditions along the Idle valley. Problems still arose when the Trent itself was affected by flood water or high tides, and under those conditions the water would back up the river and people at Retford got their feet wet. It was not until 1979 that the problem was finally solved by the building of a high capacity pumping station at West Stockwith.

East of Retford the land was also difficult to cultivate and travel was frequently impossible because of its heavy clay nature. For those seeking to develop a market town at Retford the problems of transport and communications generally must have seemed insurmountable; although they were eventually overcome, the physical nature of the surrounding land and of the town itself would for many years act to retard economic growth.

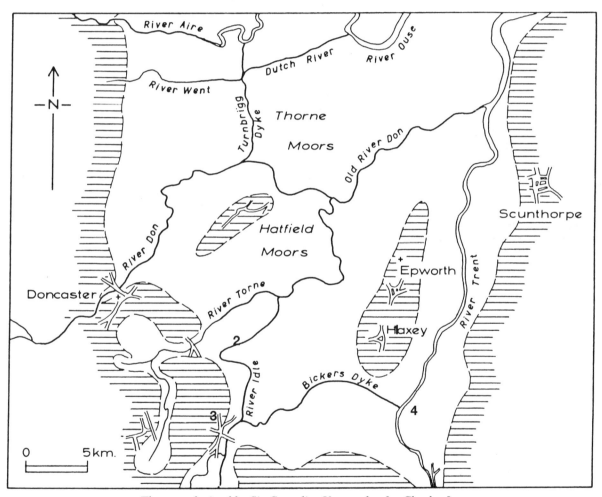

The area drained by Sir Cornelius Vermuyden for Charles I —
1 West Stockwith; 2 Idle Stop; 3 Misson and 4 Beckingham.

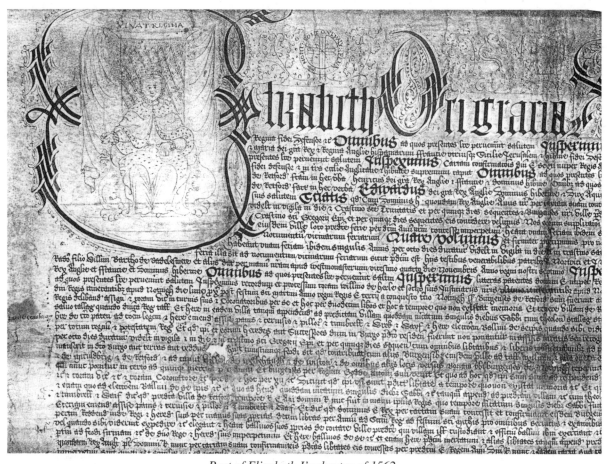

Part of Elizabeth I's charter of 1562.

East Retford's second Town Hall.

Royal Recognition

IN the Middle Ages a community could claim to be really established when the King awarded it a Royal charter. Such documents were of course in great demand because, not only did they imply Royal favour, but they also empowered the community to hold markets and fairs, collect tolls, fix local weights and measures, impose fines and assume responsibility for many other functions.

The award of a charter was recognition by the King of the ability of a community to administer its own affairs and his acceptance that it could be relied upon to make payment of its dues. In the usual way, the leading citizens of Retford petitioned the King for their charter. Invariably, if a petition was successful, the resulting document simply confirmed and legalised what was already happening, but sometimes new privileges, such as an additional fair, were granted.

As the King was responsible for raising revenue he was usually receptive to such requests as it was easier to collect rents and other dues from a legally constituted corporation than *via* the county sheriff. If the legend of Robin Hood has any basis in fact we can realise the problems faced by the Sheriff of Nottingham when collecting dues in the north of this county.

However, a charter did not automatically guarantee success and prosperity. Many places were awarded the right to hold markets and fairs but not all were able to attract enough trade. Several of the villages in the Retford area, such as Mattersey and Gringley on the Hill, at one time secured the right to hold markets but could not sustain them. At Gringley can be seen the remains of the market cross, with its stone steps on which people used to sit to sell their wares.

No one can be really positive when East Retford received its first Royal charter but it is generally agreed that in 1246 Henry III granted the town the right to hold one fair annually, to run for eight days starting on the eve of Holy Trinity (31 May). He also granted the burgesses their freedom from the payment of tolls, also of pannage (the payment of a fee for allowing one's pigs to feed in a forest) and murrage (this was a toll paid for the repair of the walls of a town, not that Retford was a walled town, but travellers through those that were had to pay the toll). The right not to pay these tolls extended, for the burgesses of East Retford, throughout the kingdom.

Retford historian John Shadrach Piercy, writing in the early 1800s, claims that an earlier charter was issued by Richard I in 1189. There is no trace of the document.

It is generally accepted that East Retford was a borough by prescription; that is by virtue of long continued or immemorial use, without interruption, of established customs and privileges. The first charter would have confirmed the town's status and made it legal; further charters re-confirmed its rights and added others.

Saturday markets in East Retford were first made legal in 1279 by the charter awarded by Edward I, but they were probably held before that. He also gave the town the right to set up stocks and a ducking stool and to commit people to them. It is said that the ducking stool was near to the present bridge in Bridgegate, using the river Idle in which to immerse the unfortunate women strapped in it. The stocks were originally set up under the steps of the first Town Hall, which stood in the market place, and were later moved to The Square.

Between fighting the Scots and the French, Edward III granted a new charter to East Retford. Dated 1336, this confirmed all previous privileges, exempted the burgesses from jury service and, most surprisingly, in view of his difficulties with France, absolved them from foreign service.

Perhaps the most important charter granted to East Retford was that of James I in 1608. This lengthy and detailed document sets out the status of the town in clear terms — *'We ordain that the said town of East Retford shall be and remain amongst other things for ever a free town of itself. That there shall be a senior bailiff chosen from the chief magistrates of the town and a junior bailiff. That there shall be twelve of the burgesses chosen as aldermen and that these persons do constitute a common council of the town. We do appoint William Thornton to be senior bailiff and Nicholas Watson junior bailiff'*. The charter ruled that the bailiffs were to be appointed annually but the aldermen were to hold office for life unless they were removed for any reasonable cause. If an alderman died his place was to be filled by a nominee of the remaining aldermen.

It was this charter which firmly established the constitution of the Corporation of East Retford and the manner in which the town was to be governed for the next 227 years. The bailiffs and aldermen were to be assisted by a recorder; that is a magistrate having limited criminal and civil jurisdiction in a city or borough and presiding over quarter sessions. He was to be appointed by them and in turn he was to appoint a town clerk. Between them they were responsible for the administration of the town and its revenues, plus the enforcement of its laws and privileges.

By the 16th century the corporations which ran towns such as East Retford were powerful, in fact the towns they controlled were almost mini-states. Provided the corporation paid its dues to the lord of the manor, which at Retford was the King, it would be left to run its own affairs with little interference by central government. There was no standard system of collecting revenue with which a corporation could carry out its functions; revenue for East Retford Corporation came from bridge tolls, market charges, fairs and property rents. The services the Corporation was required to provide were, to say the least, limited so it did not require a large income.

By securing successive charters East Retford established its independence. It was free to pursue the development of its markets and to become the natural centre of a large part of north Nottinghamshire.

The town's records are sketchy, with long periods unrecorded, so the biggest mystery appears to be why the town ever became established as a centre in the first place. Why didn't West Retford become a market town instead of the newer East Retford? What advantages did East Retford have? At first impressions it had none to compare with those with which other boroughs developed. It was not at the head of a navigable river, there was no castle or large religious establishment nearby and it was not on a major road. What was to become the Great North Road passed by several miles to the west, as did the Nottingham road.

However, it did have one road passing through it and that was the then important route to Lincoln *via* Littleborough. Travellers from Blyth, Worksop and that area, wishing to reach Lincoln, would cross the river Idle at Retford, pass along what is now Bridgegate and Chapelgate, go up Spital Hill and on to Littleborough *via* North Leverton. Neither Gainsborough nor Dunham bridges had then been built.

Another important factor in the town's favour was that its lord of the manor was the King, whereas West Retford was held by the church. The king was usually willing to rent out his rights to tolls and market dues, but the Church was less amenable.

East Retford, in its earliest years, probably was no more than a cluster of dwellings along Bridgegate leading to what we know as Cannon Square. Here the road forked, the route to Littleborough being more or less straight ahead, while that to the left went to Moorgate and Clarborough. At what is now White Hart corner a further road led off to the right to modern Carolgate, originally known as Carr Hill Gate. The present Grove Street and The Square did not exist; neither did Exchange Street or the other roads which now seem so much a part of the town.

As the markets attracted more people so it became necessary to make room for an increased number of stalls and that was achieved by widening the Bridgegate end of the road leading to Carolgate, so as to create a market place, which is the name it still bears. Here in 1388 was built the first town hall, a long building mostly of wood. At ground level were the shambles, the stalls from which butchers sold meat and poultry. Above was the hall itself with its six unglazed windows, fitted with iron bars and shutters; a flight of steps led to the main door and under these were the stocks.

The roof of the town hall had heavy slates and a cupola in which was hung the town bell. This was rung to summon people to the court sessions and to announce the commencement of trading on every market day. Anyone who started to sell goods before the bell had rung would find themselves in serious trouble. Apparently in 1754 the Corporation decided that its ancient town hall had reached the end of its useful life and had it demolished to make room for a new and grander structure. The foundation stone was laid in 1755 and the finished building retained the arrangement of stalls for the market below the first floor meeting rooms.

East Retford's second town hall was a handsome building. It had two imposing meeting rooms; the larger of these was 70ft long and 26ft wide with a raised bench at one end for visiting judges and the magistrates at court sessions. This room was generally known as the Moot Hall and was used for public meetings and other large gatherings. Leading off the Moot Hall was the Council Room, 20ft by 26ft, used for meetings of the Corporation and as a magistrates' court on alternate Saturdays. Over the ornate fireplace hung a full-length portrait of James I, presented to the Corporation by the Duke of Newcastle.

The southern exterior of the building had a triangular pediment in the style of the period and to this was fixed the town's armorial bearings, a shield with two falcons. At the northern end was a twin flight of steps curving gracefully to the main entrance and down these on civic occasions, such as when they attended a service at the parish church, the members of the Corporation would begin their procession. Wearing their robes of purple, trimmed with fur, the bailiffs and aldermen, headed by the two Sergeants at Mace, the Town Crier and the Town Clerk would walk slowly through the town as if to demonstrate their almost absolute authority.

When the Corporation entertained in the Town Hall it used its impressive collection of civic plate. Food would be eaten off gold plates and wine drunk from fine goblets. At the installation of a new Lord High Steward the entertaining would be on a lavish scale with banquets lasting until late at night. The names of those who held that office make an imposing list and include successive Earls of Shrewsbury and many Dukes of Newcastle. It was the latter who for many years exercised considerable influence upon the town and its Corporation, and not always to its advantage.

While such pomp may have enhanced the standing of the Corporation it did little to improve the lot of more lowly residents. There was no proper water supply or means of sanitation, living conditions for many were appalling and outbreaks of fever commonplace. But East Retford was not alone in this, as most English towns cared little for social welfare until the reforms of the 1830s.

A sun-dappled view of West Retford's Broad Stone.

Nottinghamshire in the mid-18th century.

Retford, Redford, or East Retford, is an Antient Burough, enjoying many privileges granted to it by several of the Kings of England. King James 1st Incorporated it by the Name of Bailiffs, and Burgesses, with 12 Aldermen, they have also two Chamberlains, a Town Clerk, & two Serjants at Mace. Here is a Free Grammar School, and a commodious Town-Hall, in which the Sessions for the Town and County are held; and the Shambles under it are the best in the County. The Market is famous for Hops and Barley for Malt. There are also large Hop-grounds or Plantations for Hops, in the Neighbourhood of this Town. This place bears the Name of East Retford, because it stands on the East side of the River Idle, and is joined by a Stone-Bridge to West Retford, which tho' it seems to be a part of the same Town, is another Parish; in which there's nothing remarkable but its fine Hospital, founded by John Dorrel Dr. of Physick. An: Dom: 1666. within a mile of East Retford there's a Well called St. Johns Well, famous for great Cures effected by its Water which is remarkably cold.

Extract from the 18th century map.

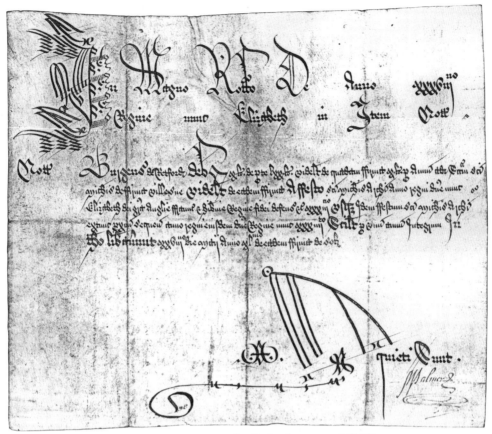

A receipt for East Retford's fee farm rent, 1596/6.

Edward III's 1372 Retford charter.

Wilson's Windmill, Caledonian Road, 1910.

East Retford's Broad Stone.

Bridgegate Bridge, the site of Retford's watermill.

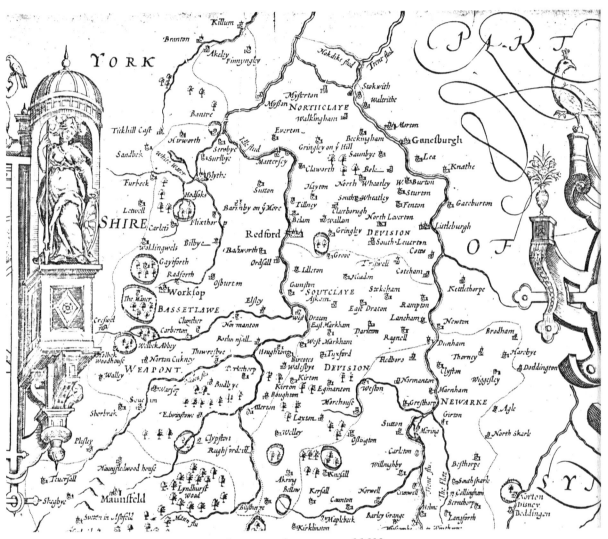

An extract from a map of 1610.

For Divine Service

RETFORD has many features pleasing to the eye and not the least of these are its two parish churches. Both have a long history and both have played a major role in the life of the community.

St Swithun's, the parish church of East Retford, is also known as the Corporation church due to its long association with successive town councils, mayors, aldermen and councillors. It still has its Corporation pew, carved with the emblem of the Borough of East Retford, with the Mayor's seat partitioned from the rest. This is furnished with a highly polished brass lectern and has a special fitting to hold the mace. There is no longer a Borough of East Retford but the Town Mayor and the Charter Trustees still occupy the pew on civic occasions.

Architecturally, St Swithun's fulfils everyone's expectations of how the parish church of an English country town should appear — a grey stone tower topped with battlements and pinnacles, high pointed windows in the Gothic style filled with stained glass, a deep, cool entrance porch and all surrounded by neatly mown lawns and mature trees. Inside can be found a list of vicars beginning in 1317 when John de Sutton was the incumbent and many memorials to past citizens of Retford and those who held positions of responsibility. Among those remembered is Sir Wharton Amcotts, whose memorial tablet tells us that prior to his death in 1807 he 'represented this respectable Borough in Parliament for 20 years'. Past aldermen, town clerks, bailiffs, solicitors and bankers are among many are the names recorded.

Located at the junction of the old roads to Littleborough and Gainsborough, the church is flanked by Georgian town houses and the older Sun Inn. As if for protection it is fronted by a cannon that was last fired by the Russians during the Battle of Sebastopol and brought back to Retford as a trophy in 1859. That is overseen by the stucco-fronted former Crown Hotel, which itself was the victim of many skirmishes during East Retford's more riotous elections.

Although the present church has such a pleasing look of antiquity it is not the first to have stood on this site but is the result of several rebuildings. The first reference to St Swithun's was made in 1258 when the then Archbishop of York gave it to a chapel of that city, but since then it has had a chequered history. In 1528 a serious fire destroyed much of East Retford and badly damaged the church as well. At that time the town was made up of thatched, timber-framed buildings and, when a fire broke out, there was little that could he done to contain it.

Following the fire, extensive re-building of the church took place but apparently the town failed to keep it in good repair as in 1651 a severe gale demolished the tower and the chancel, leaving the building in a ruinous state. It remained so for several years until the Corporation of East Retford came to the rescue, and raised the money, by various means including the sale of property, to rebuild at a cost of £1,500. Unfortunately, in its zeal to restore, the Corporation disposed of some property that it only held in trust, part of the endowment of the Grammar School, and that led to a legal battle which was to occupy the minds of lawyers and towns-people for nearly two hundred years.

Until the Reformation there were two chantry chapels attached to the church, founded by the bailiffs and burgesses of East Retford Corporation in the 1300s. They were known as the Trinity and Our Lady chantries and their endowments provided for the support of two priests, whose principal role was to say prayers for the souls of the departed benefactors and their families. By 1548 all chantries had been suppressed and East Retford's chapels would have been destroyed either by the great fire or during re-building. However, one of them was rebuilt in 1873, this time to the left of the chancel, and re-opened by the Bishop of Lincoln for the general use of the congregation.

At night the mellow stones of the church bask in the warm glow of floodlighting and, when the bell ringers are making their music, the whole town seems to smile.

At West Retford the parish church of St Michael, standing on its slight hill, gives the appearance of holding itself aloof from the bustle and noise of markets and fairs. To leave Bridgegate and enter the quiet serenity of the churchyard is to pass into an older, more placid age. Visually, St Michael's greatest contribution to the appearance of the town is its beautiful tower and spire. Dating from the 14th century, this is a prominent landmark that seems to float above the town.

West Retford's list of rectors begins in 1227 and throughout the centuries the church has been the core of its parish, administering charities, almshouses and schools long before the state became interested in such matters. No doubt most of those whose names appear on the list of rectors served the parish well, but it is always the most eccentric who are remembered.

Perhaps the best known is Reverend Henry Dickenson, awarded the living in 1837 by East Retford Borough Council — patron of the parish in succession to the old Corporation. Henry Dickenson was related to the wealthy family of that name who lived at West Retford Hall. They were closely associated with the political views of the 4th Duke of Newcastle and, as he was the Lord High Steward of the Borough, some influence may have been brought to bear upon the Council when it decided this appointment.

Reverend Henry Dickenson quickly gained a reputation for extreme meanness, but it is difficult be sure who was the most frugal between him and his wife. One of many stories told is that on market days they would walk into town, where she would argue and haggle with the stallholders over prices. While she was so engaged the rector would slip into a baker's shop to buy a cake, which he would surreptitiously eat before she spotted him.

Although West Retford did not become part of the Borough until 1878, the Corporation became involved with St Michael's as early as 1658, when the patronage passed into its hands. This must have evoked mixed feelings among the people of East Retford, for at that time St Michael's was in a sorry state, and had to be re-roofed in 1686.

Two years after the abolition of the old Corporation the new Council decided to sell the advowson of the rectory of West Retford and ordered the Town Clerk to advertise it, at a minimum price of £3,000. No buyers were forthcoming and in 1838 further instructions were given to re-advertise in the London *Times*, *Chronicle* and *Standard* in addition to county newspapers, this time at £2,000. The highest offer received was £1,600, which was declined. However, in due course a proposal from John Hood Esq. of Nettleham was accepted, in the sum of £2,005.

What John Hood thought about the behaviour of rector Dickenson remains a mystery, but however much he may have disapproved there was little he could do. Twenty years later Dickenson was still in residence and making sure everyone knew where 'his property' began, by having a tablet put on to a wall at Bridgegate to tell them. It is still there.

ONLY a mile or so away from East Retford market square is the ancient church of All Hallows, which has served Ordsall for over 700 years. Although that village has been engulfed by the town, it was not officially incorporated within the old borough until 1878, and the church never came under its influence. With the River Idle flowing between the two places, Ordsall has always managed to retain a separate identity.

Although Ordsall is listed in Domesday there is no evidence that either Saxons or Normans built an early church. The present building dates from about 1250 but has been considerably altered and extended, with major restoration in 1877. That was when considerations of comfort brought pews with sloping backs.

Fortunately the restorers did not destroy the beautiful rood screen, which has been in the church since the mid-1400s. It survived the Reformation, even though it was banished from the chancel and kept at the base of the tower until the 1930s, when it returned to its rightful place. Also to survive was an interesting wall monument which has a kneeling figure dressed in Elizabethan costume and dates from 1603. It is a memorial to Samuel Bevercotes, who was a former lord of the manor and it too was banished from public gaze until a more sympathetic rector removed it from the belfry, where it had been hidden for over a hundred years, and put it back at the side of the nave.

Two of Retford's best-known family names are recorded in Ordsall Church. One is that of Denman, now best known by the public library in the town. The Denmans played a major part in the history and development of Retford and at Ordsall they provided a rector. William Denman was first appointed rector of Ordsall in 1550 but was deprived of the living during the brief reign of the Catholic Queen Mary, because of his Protestant beliefs. However, when Elizabeth succeeded he was reinstated and looked after the parish for a further 29 years.

A window records the other well-known name, is that of John Shadrach Piercy, who is best remembered for his history of Retford, published in 1828. He held a variety of posts, including that of school teacher, newspaper correspondent and parish clerk. For a short while he was an elected councillor of East Retford Borough Council, but lost office when he ceased to be a ratepayer; a legal requirement in the 1800s.

As West Retford Church is crowned by its spire so Ordsall has its tower. The lower part was built in the 1300s and the upper a hundred years later. During the 1877 restoration the battlements and pinnacles were taken down and rebuilt and soon after three more bells were added to bring the peal to six.

The rapid growth of Retford in the 1800s brought the need for more churches. St Saviour's, built in 1829 to serve Moorgate, was the first, and this was followed in 1898 by proposals to erect St Alban's on London Road.

Although Babworth, Scrooby and other villages in north Nottinghamshire were to provide members of the group now famous as the Pilgrim Fathers, none came from Retford itself. However, there were others who separated from the established church, such as James Parnell, who was to become the first Quaker martyr. He was born at East Retford in 1636 and at the age of seventeen came under the influence of George Fox. He died for his convictions in 1653 in Colchester prison, as a result of barbarous treatment.

The Baptist movement came to Retford as early as the 1600s and a chapel existed at West Retford in 1776. Their numbers steadily increased and a chapel of 1815 was replaced by the present larger one in 1872. It was the Baptists' practice of holding open-air baptisms in the canal near Retford town lock which created their perhaps most unwelcome publicity. The ceremony involves total submersion and this caused delay to working boats. Boatmen expressed their annoyance in language not fitting for the occasion and eventually services were held in the privacy of the chapel. In one respect the Baptists of Retford were years ahead of their time for, in the 1800s, they set up several workshops at the back of their chapel, for the use of unemployed tradesmen who wanted to trade on their own account.

The imposing Methodist church which dominates Grove Street provides clear evidence of how successful that movement became in Retford. While the exterior is impressive, inside can be found everything that one expects of a Methodist church built at the peak of the movement's popularity. The elevated centre pulpit, with its brass lectern and rails, is backed by a magnificent display of organ pipes, a gracefully curving gallery and decked pews, all combine to create a sense of theatre. Surely no preacher could fail to be inspired by such a setting and no congregation not join wholeheartedly in the singing of the stirring hymns for which Methodists are deservedly famous.

Grove Street Methodist church was built in 1879 and stands on the site of an earlier, but much smaller chapel of 1823. This could seat 600 people but even that was not enough; its successor provides 1,000 sittings and gives everyone a clear view of the pulpit. A feature of any Methodist building is the number of foundation stones that can be seen, each bearing the name of the person responsible for laying it. When the time came for the laying of the foundation stones of the present Grove Street church, it was decided to make the occasion a major town event. This auspicious ceremony was on 30 October 1879 and it was attended by the Mayor, together with the other members of the Corporation. At 11am precisely the first stone was laid, followed by several others, silver trowels were presented and then everyone walked in procession to the Town Hall. Several more ceremonies took place when the church was opened the following year.

All this pomp was somewhat different from the scenes John Wesley had endured in 1779 when he first preached in Retford outside the old town hall. A rowdy group had gathered to disrupt the meeting but were kept in order by some Wesleyan supporters, led by a certain John Mackfarland. He was no stranger to violence and at the time was a new convert to Methodism from a more aggressive lifestyle.

Mackfarland was of unkempt appearance and rough manners. He arrived in Retford when the Chesterfield Canal was being constructed in 1776 and obtained manual work with one of the contractors. When the canal was completed he stayed, first as a boatman and later as a coal merchant and shopkeeper. He failed to achieve success in either, perhaps because his preoccupation with Methodism overtook his attention to business matters.

He had promised John Wesley he would build a chapel in Retford. He borrowed £100 to erect, partly with his own hands, a small chapel on what was then known at Rosemary Lane, but is now called Spa Lane, off Carolgate. It was licensed for worship in 1781 and was extremely plain and austere, with backless benches and a rail down the centre of the building to keep the sexes separate, ensuring they 'did not sit together promiscuously during divine service'.

By 1789 Mackfarland's chapel had been replaced by a larger one built on the same site, but that was also outgrown by 1823 when land was acquired in Grove Street (then known as Newgate Street). John Mackfarland was present at the stone-laying ceremony but he was no longer a lusty young man, ready to fight anyone who attempted to disrupt proceedings. Old age and poverty had overtaken him and he was

22

The Book of Retford

living as a pauper at the nearby workhouse. He had been offered a place in the Trinity Hospital, where he would have been well cared for, but this he refused as he would have been obliged to attend services at the parish church, which he likened to 'selling his soul to the devil for a place'.

Although the Methodist movement was flourishing it was not without internal dissension and in 1818 a Primitive Methodist group was formed. In 1841 they purchased a former theatre in Carolgate, which became known as the Swingboat chapel because of its unusual shape. This was demolished in 1870 and the foundation stones of the new one laid. Perhaps not with the same display of civic pomp as at Grove Street, but nevertheless 1,000 people took part in a procession from the Corn Exchange, and tea was later served there to 750 of them.

Various other Methodist splinter groups set up their own places of worship during the 1800's, each of them devoutly convinced that their interpretation of the Lord's message and of how it should be taught was the correct one. Not only did Methodists but several other denominations fervently raised funds so that they could hold services in purpose-built chapels instead of in borrowed rooms or the open air. The effect of all this upon a small town like Retford was considerable. With a church or chapel on virtually every road, each with its Sunday school, religion — or at least the observance of it — dominated. Not that church or chapel attendance meant that the social distinctions were lessened, for the differences of class were maintained by the pews that people were permitted to occupy. As most of them were rented, there could be no question of anyone getting 'ideas above their station'.

At Retford, as everywhere, the social changes brought about by two world wars resulted in a dramatic fall in attendances. Most of the smaller places of worship could no longer be maintained and had to be closed; some, such as the Carolgate chapel, were demolished; shops now occupy their sites. Fortunately many remain to contribute architecturally, if no longer spiritually, to the town. Buildings that used to echo to lusty hymn-singing or the orations of devout preachers now see many other uses. Perhaps the most ignominious of them all involved the former Congregational church on Carolgate bridge which, for several years, was used as a nightclub with a style of entertainment that earned it notoriety over a wide area and attracted many whose behaviour made them unwelcome.

It has not been downhill for all religious denominations during the 20th century, for the Roman Catholics were able to build a brand-new church on Babworth Road. Its opening in 1959 meant that, for the first time in over 400 years, they could hold a Catholic mass in their own purpose-built church.

It is still possible to capture the atmosphere and fervour which prevailed at the height of the Methodist movement, by attending a concert at their Grove Street church, when the Retford Male Voice Choir, accompanied by the organ and a guest brass band, lead the 1,000-strong audience in the singing of a favourite hymn such as Jerusalem. On such occasions the old building, with its perfect acoustics, comes alive in the same way that it did every Sunday for so many years.

The Corporation church of East Retford — St Swithun's.

The 1870 Carolgate Chapel of the Primitive Methodists, built on the site of the 'swingboat' chapel.

St Michael's, parish church of West Retford — the Galway Arms is in the background.

Ordsall Church shows an absence of symmetry often found in Nottinghamshire churches.

The proud symbol of Methodism — the ornate chapel on Grove Street.

The Baptist Church, Hospital Road.

The former Congregational Chapel on Carolgate Bridge.

St Saviour's, Moorgate, the first of Retford's newer Anglican Churches.

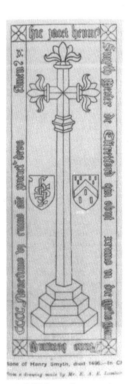

A 1496 tombstone in East Retford Church.

Borough of East Retford.

A SCHEDULE of the Rents, Dues and Payments arising from, and payable in respect of, the Fairs, Markets, Stallages, and Shambles of East Retford, belonging to the Corporation.

		s.	d.
STANDAGE for HOP WAGGONS each		1	0
Ditto CARTS ditto		0	6
Ditto CHEESE WAGGONS ditto		1	0
Ditto CARTS ditto		0	6

These Charges to include the Weighing of Hops and Cheese.

		s.	d.
POTATOES—Cart Load (Horse)		0	4
Ditto (Ass)		0	2
Sack and Barrow each		0	1
SHEEP PENS—In the Market, according to the quantity of Sheep, each		0 6 to 0 8	
Ditto In the Sheep Fair, each		1	0
PIG PENS—When Pens found		0	4
Ditto When not found		0	2
BUTCHER'S STALLS—Non-residents each		1	4
Ditto Residents		0	8
Ditto Freemen		0	4

The Butchers to find their own Stalls and Boards, but the Corporation to set them out.

		s.	d.
FISH STALLS—Per Week		1	0

The Parties using the Stalls to set them out.

		s.	d.
OTHER STALLS—Non-residents, per yard		0	5
Ditto Residents, ditto		0	2½
Ditto Freemen, ditto		0	1

The Corporation to find Stalls and Boards, and to set them out.

		s.	d.
BUTTER, POULTRY AND EGG STALLS— Each No. per week		0	1
POTTER'S STANDINGS as now used, each		1	4
COOPER'S STANDINGS ditto, ditto		0	9
CHAIR-MAKER'S ditto, ditto		0	3
OTHER STANDINGS for every 10 square yards		0	4
SHAMBLES—For every single Stall per annum, payable 6 months in advance		~~15~~	~~0~~
For cleaning the Shambles, in addition, per annum		1	0
WEIGHING MEAT—Butchers renting a Stall a Day.		0	1
Other parties, for a Beast		1	0
Calf		0	6
Pig		0	3
Sheep		0	2

No Charge is made for Corn, Fruit (on the Ground), Carts, Waggons, Beasts, or Horses standing in the Market.

By Order of the Council,

W. NEWTON, TOWN CLERK.

Town Clerk's Office, September 1, 1843.

HODSON, PRINTER, RETFORD.

Retford Market schedule of dues for 1843.

Of Markets and Mills

RETFORD is now, just as it always has been, a market town. It was to hold a market that the ancient charters were first obtained. Today's markets are tame affairs by comparison; they have no cattle charging round the Square, no live poultry, no pens containing sheep, lambs or pigs and none of the noise and smells that went with them. In fact the most pungent aroma at today's markets is that of fried onions wafting from the hot dog stall. But the importance of the markets to the town is no less than it has ever been, for without them Retford's trade would decline; compare the bustle and crowds of market days to those when no stalls fill the Square.

The true market place is not the Square but the area to the east that has shops on one side and the White Hart on the other. Through the middle of this ran a track that led to Carolgate and the Commons, on each side of which stalls were set up. Close to hand was the old town hall, with the meat market, or Shambles as it was known, beneath it. Hanging in a cupola on top of the town hall was a bell that was rung to announce the opening of the market; it was strictly forbidden to commence trading before the bell had been tolled.

When the markets first began the Square was nothing more than open land leading to the water meadows alongside the river Idle. It was probably used as a convenient space on which to put cattle and horses, brought to town to be sold. As the importance of Retford market increased and its residents became wealthier the Square became a highly desirable area, around which elegant town houses were eventually built during the Georgian era.

It was the re-routing of the Great North Road through Retford in 1766 that resulted in Carolgate becoming the major north/south through road in place of the older way that had branched off Churchgate towards Dominie Cross Roads. The extra traffic caused severe problems on market days and traders had to make more use of the Square, this trend strengthened by the Corporation's determination to make the town the centre of the region for the sale of livestock.

Nowadays, when people talk of fairs they mean dodgem cars, big wheels and fast-moving roundabouts, all brightly illuminated and with amplified music. In earlier years, fairs were annual events held for a specific purpose and often marking important religious dates. At Retford fairs were held for selling sheep, horses, cattle and hops. The sheep fairs began in 1753 and in later years were held on Spa Common; from 1843 the horse fairs took place along Grove Street and these were notoriously lively affairs which attracted dealers and gypsies from a wide area. Anyone thinking of buying would walk along the rows of tethered horses which were of all ages, size and temperament. At the slightest sign of interest the dealers would gallop their horses furiously up and down Grove Street to prove their fitness, before commencing the haggling and hard bargaining that was an essential element of every sale.

Every fair attracted its quota of peddlers, buskers and pavement traders, not forgetting pickpockets and snatch thieves and, as the inns were open from early in the morning, there would be many the worse for drink. On a quieter note were swings, sideshows and roundabouts, forerunners of present-day funfairs.

The fairs held in Retford nowadays are the direct descendants of those that have been held for hundreds of years, although they no longer have any connection with the sale of livestock. They have been kept alive by traditional showmen's families such as the Tubys of Doncaster, one of whom rose to become Mayor of that town, though whether he abandoned his caravan to live at the Mansion House is not recorded. The right to hold a fair in Retford was kept alive throughout the last war by an elderly Mrs Tuby, who would always arrive on the due dates to set up a small stall. Those who now complain about the traffic disruption created by the fairs should remember that they are not only keeping alive old traditions but also continuing their custom of helping the less fortunate, by giving free rides to many charitable organisations.

In spite of the apparent chaos and often unruly behaviour that the fairs and markets used to bring, they were all strictly controlled by the Corporation of East Retford through its paid official, the Sergeant at Mace. It was his duty to see that all the rules governing the market were kept and that all the payments due to the Corporation, such as tolls, stall rents and other charges, were received. Until the establishment of a police force he was responsible for seeing that the bye-laws were observed and law and order kept. Anyone who transgressed was quickly hauled before the town magistrates and, if found guilty, given immediate and public punishment. During the 1800s it was by no means uncommon for a person to be dragged from the Court out into the market place where he or she (there was no leniency shown to the women) would be stripped to the waist, tied to the back of a cart and whipped through the town 'until their backs be bloody'. Pregnant women were given some consideration, for their whipping would be deferred until after the baby was born. Up to the 1600s offenders of both sexes were stripped naked before being whipped.

For those convicted of stealing, the punishment was to be branded on the hand with a red hot iron; formerly they were branded on the face, until it became clear that those so treated were unlikely to find employment and therefore become a charge upon the parish. Retford also had its pillory and stocks in the market place; those placed in the former stood up to have garbage thrown at them, whereas in the stocks they had the luxury of sitting down.

Many a person was sentenced to be transported by the Retford magistrates, such as Charles Bailey, a butcher ordered to be 'transported for seven years to His Majesty's plantations or colonies in America for stealing one hempen sack value 10d, the property of James Bingham'. They might as well have said 'for life' because few returned home. A third of them died on the voyage to America and few lived to complete their sentence; those that did were fortunate if they could raise the cost of the fare home or manage to work their passage back. If that seems harsh it should be remembered that the theft of anything valued at more than 10d (4p) incurred the death sentence. Hangings were carried out at Retford until that unpleasant task was transferred to Nottingham.

In 1837 George Parker Suter was appointed Sergeant at Mace, Clerk of the Market and Superintendent of the Day and Night Police at an annual salary of £10 and he was reminded by the Mayor of the 'propriety of his wearing a Hat and Cloak as befitted his station'. In common with the Town Crier he was provided with a uniform by the Corporation; it was renewed annually by whichever of the town's tailors succeeded in winning the contract — there is nothing new about competitive tendering. Suter held the post until he died in 1843, whereupon the Corporation reduced the salary to £5 per annum as there was less work to do.

Retford Corporation, which depended upon revenue from the markets and property rents until the rating system was reformed, remained determined to develop them by creating new fairs and cattle markets. In 1840 a fortnightly cattle market was begun on Spa Common as well as two additional cattle fairs, stall rents in the Butter Market were reduced and consideration was given to building a corn exchange.

When news came of plans to build a railway line to the town, the Borough Council expressed its support, but was concerned that improved communications could bring increased competition.

However, in 1859 the Council received a deputation from the Great Northern and the Manchester, Sheffield and Lincolnshire railway companies to discuss the possibilities of establishing a 'Great North of England Cattle Market' near the railway station. This scheme was no doubt welcomed by those who lived in the houses around the Square who, forgetting that the town's affluence was derived from the market, frequently complained about the presence of cattle virtually on their doorsteps. Six years later the Retford Cattle Company was holding its markets on the new site at Ordsall, but the sheep fair was still held on Spa Common until the 1970s.

Eventually the competition feared by the Council in 1847 took effect and all livestock trading at Retford ceased, but it was motor transport, not the railways, which brought it to an end. The general market continues to flourish and market gardeners and poultry keepers still bring their fresh produce to sell.

Although the great industrial revolution left Retford virtually unscathed the town has never been entirely without workshops and machinery. Perhaps its first industrial activity was that of milling. There were water mills on either side of the river Idle at Bridgegate as early as 1086. Used to grind corn, they were granted to Welbeck Abbey in 1227 for an annual rent payable to the King, but eventually became the property of the Corporation of East Retford. Other water mills existed at Ordsall and Bolham and they were the first to be put to a new and more profitable use, that of paper-making. By 1856 West Retford mill had also been converted to make paper and in 1866 Mr Ben Haigh began building his Albert Road mill.

Ben Haigh was apparently a resourceful person for he acted as his own architect and personally supervised the building of the mill, together with the installation of the machinery. His stepfather, Mr J.H. Waddington, was also a paper manufacturer at the Ordsall and Retford mills. Albert Road mill was, from its beginning, powered by steam, with coal supplies brought by canal boats that could moor alongside. On 11 August 1887 a serious fire destroyed the main portion of the mill but this was rebuilt and in 1922 the business was purchased by the Remington Kraft Paper Company. After they went into liquidation in 1930 ownership passed to a German-based company called Erfurt, in conjunction with Spicers Limited, who at the time were paper handlers. When the war came and German property in Britain was expropriated Spicers took over sole ownership. In 1963 Spicers were absorbed by the Reed Paper Group.

Steam power posed a serious threat to the water mills and eventually they were also fitted with boilers and chimneys. This was generally welcomed by local people, particularly with regard to the Bridgegate mills, as it meant that the shuttles which held back the river water could be removed, thus solving the flooding problem. The owners of West Retford Hall, the Huntsmans, were less enthusiastic and in 1875 complained bitterly to the Corporation about the 'nuisance of smoke from Mr Waddington's paper mill in Bridgegate'. The fact that the Huntsmans' fortune was derived from their huge smelting works, which polluted much of Sheffield, was obviously irrelevant. By 1881 the problem had ceased to exist, for the mill was no longer working and the Council was considering plans to demolish all the buildings and remove the mill races.

Retford also had several windmills, one of them at Spital Hill and owned in 1826 by John Holmes; a road of that name now occupies its site. Poplar Street, off Thrumpton Lane, was where a five storeyed smock mill with four sails must have made an impressive sight, but its various owners, including a Mayor of East Retford, lost their money and were declared bankrupt. The old mill was finally purchased by the Northern Rubber Company in 1902 by which time it was derelict. South Retford windmill appears to have been rather more successful and, in an effort to keep up with the times, installed steam machinery in the 1890s, but milling had ceased by 1929. It stood between Caledonian Road and the railway. Storcroft Mill was also near Caledonian Road; it was built in 1866 and ended its life in 1904 when it was destroyed by fire.

It was Retford's position in the centre of a large corn-growing area which created the need for so many mills. The corn harvest was brought to the town's market to sell and it was easier to grind it there than incur the costs of carting it away, especially after the canal was built and the boats could carry away the flour. In turn, the presence of so many mills created the need for machinery and that led to the setting up of several engineering works to make and repair it. Of these the most successful was that of Charles Hopkinson, whose Beehive Works were employing over 200 men by 1895; they were taken over by W.J. Jenkins in 1896. Here was made the machinery for the new roller mills that were to make the old wind and water mills unprofitable.

Milling was not Retford's only early industry; perhaps the one which today appears the most illogical is that of sail making. Why sails were made so far from the nearest harbour seems hard to understand until it is remembered that all the boats on the Trent used sails and West Stockwith and Gainsborough were both busy ports. Even the narrow boats of the Chesterfield Canal were equipped with sails for river work. Another use for sailcloth was on the early windmills, before the more familiar wooden slatted sweeps were invented.

Sailcloth, coarse linen and tent cloth were made from the fibre of flax, a crop which was widely grown in Nottinghamshire but is seldom seen nowadays. Several factors led to the decline of sail making in Retford, such as the advent of steam power, the cheapness of imported flax and the popularity of cotton. One company remains, that of Mudford and Sons, which was established in 1832 when it made ropes and twines, and is now a leading tent and marquee contractor.

If an ambitious enterprise that was begun in 1788 had succeeded, Retford could have become a mill town, perhaps even another Bradford. The enterprise was that of Major John Cartwright's Revolution Mill, a huge wool-spinning and weaving factory that covered a site of some ten acres. By 1790 the mill employed six hundred, but it was never profitable and soon closed. No offers to purchase were made and eventually its buildings and equipment were sold piecemeal at an auction held at the White Hart, leaving its six hundred employees to find other work.

Retford's thriving market created the demand for a great variety of goods, and early directories list such trades as hat makers, boot and shoe makers, saddlers, maltsters, bankers, brewers, watch and clock makers, stay makers, tinners and many, many more. It seems that Retford could supply most needs and services, and prospered as a result.

Market Place, Retford on a quiet day early this century, when Miss Hirst of Moorgate Villa received this card, inviting her to meet there at 2.30pm.

Cannon Square today — but perhaps once the earliest market place in town.

Cars parked at will in the 1930s Market Place and Square.

The Shambles was the marketplace for Retford's meat trade — built as part of the Town Hall complex and subsequently demolished.

Tanner's Coals' 'Grate Stuff' in the 1930s.

John White offered reasonably priced wines and spirits.

Another use for part of the Shambles — the Fire Brigade HQ, with its sturdy double doors.

*In 1889 watches and clocks were
seriously advertised.*

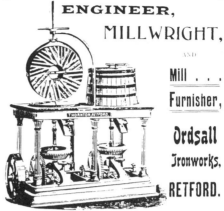

*Joseph Thornton was a prominent Ordsall
engineer and millwright.*

The last stagecoach outing — probably a revival — c1908, and about to leave The Square.

Retford   R.D.C.   Grove Street. Retford.
Ancott House

Messrs. Henry Spencer & Sons

(Partners—Harry A. Spencer, F.A.I., Eric C. Spencer, M.B.E., M.A. (Agriculture) Cantab., F.R.I.C.S.,
Chartered Surveyor, F.A.I., Rupert Wallis Spencer, M.A. (Agriculture) Cantab., F.A.I.)

AUCTIONEERS, VALUERS & LAND AGENTS.

OFFICES—20, The Square, Retford; Telephone No. 531/2;
91, Bridge Street, Worksop;   „   „   2654;
9, Norfolk Row, Sheffield 1;   „   „   25206;
Also at Retford, Worksop and Mansfield Cattle Markets on Market Days.

1 Rover Car	80	-	-	
Comm.	£4			
Toll	1s			
Adv. (Retford Times)	6s	4 7 -	75 13 -	

Henry Spencer & Sons send their statement to East Retford RDC after selling a second-hand Rover.

The original route of the Great North Road is clearly marked on this pre-1750 map;
it goes well to the west of Retford.

The 1801 map shows the new route, taking the Great North Road, and its more than welcome trade, through the town centre. The old road is still marked, and so is the other main trade artery — the Chesterfield Canal.

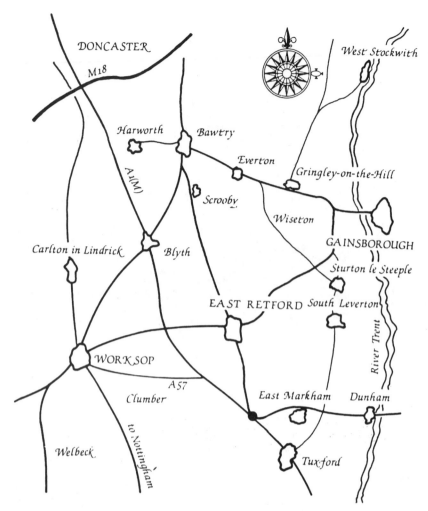

*A modern map shows the Great North Road as the A1;
as the car strangled trade, so the road was moved yet again.*

Whitehouses, c1904, where the 'new' route once took the Great North Road to Retford.

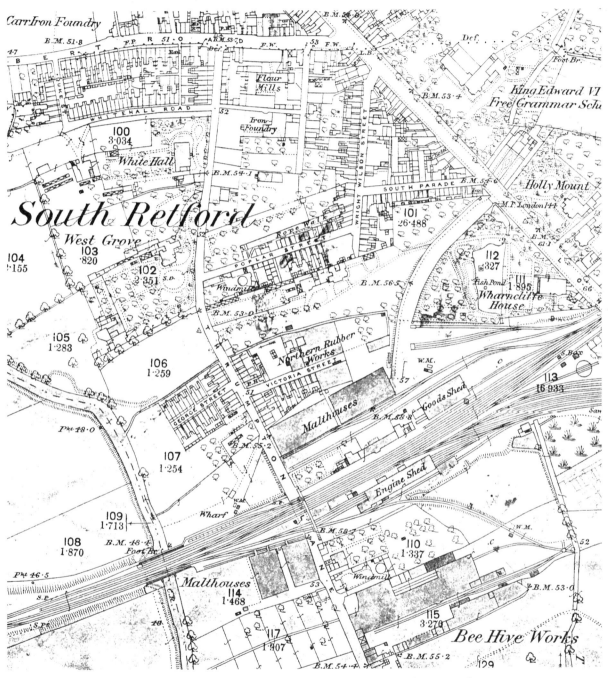

The Manchester, Sheffield and Lincolnshire Railway has arrived.

Sailing barges on the Trent were rigged and clothed by Retford.

An aqueduct of 1776 carried the Canal over the river Idle at Retford.

Grove Street Mill stood beside the Chesterfield Canal.

A former furniture warehouse at Retford.

Retford canal basin with the original Corporation warehouse on the right — built in 1777.

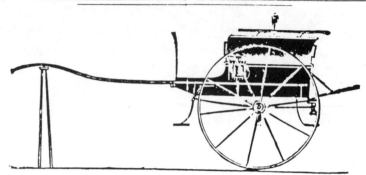

An early billhead.

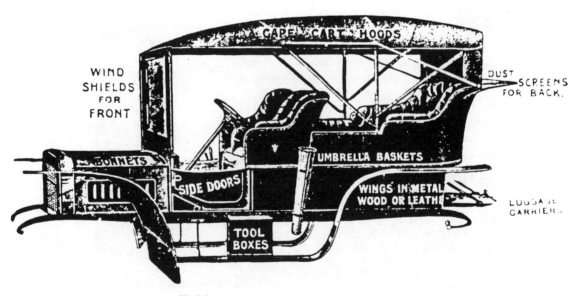

W. Silver, Borough Carriage and Motor Works.

The Way Forward

NO market town could hope to flourish unless it had good communications. Retford got off to rather a bad start as its only road of any consequence was the one which led to Littleborough and the river Idle was not navigable beyond Bawtry.

Prior to 1776 Retford had looked upon Bawtry with envy because of its position at the head of the River Idle Navigation, which gave access to the port of West Stockwith on the river Trent. Although little more than a village, Bawtry was extremely prosperous, with wealthy merchants' houses lining its streets. It was the nearest place to the growing industries of South Yorkshire, from which goods could be exported and long trains of heavily loaded pack horses were a common sight as they made their slow and laborious way to the wharf.

The Corporation of East Retford and its supporters believed that, if a river wharf could be established in their town, it would capture much of Bawtry's trade. Unfortunately, the river between the two places was shallow in summer and subject to flooding in wet seasons; it also followed a particularly winding and tortuous course, with tight hairpin bends, making passage for all but the smallest boat impossible. In spite of those disadvantages a serious attempt was made to make the Idle navigable in 1720, when the Corporation sponsored an Act of Parliament which gave them the necessary powers. In the same year a lock was built at Bolham on a by-pass channel near the watermill but, either through lack of money or of enthusiasm, little else was done. Cargo-carrying boats never reached Retford *via* the River Idle, and Bolham lock remains to this day a monument to failed endeavour.

Efforts to revive the scheme were made in 1757 to no effect. Perhaps this was due to the greater attraction of the Great North Road, which passed Retford a few miles to the west. Its traffic was rapidly increasing, much to the economic benefit of Tuxford and of the Bell Inn at Barnby Moor. Tuxford was also a market town and becoming a greater potential threat to Retford. Perhaps it was the ignominy of having to send to Tuxford or the Rushey Inn for its mail that goaded Retford into petitioning Parliament to have the road diverted through the town. Although petitioning began in 1757 success was not achieved until 1766, when an Act was passed which authorised the construction of a road from Markham Moor through Retford to Barnby Moor, where it linked with the original route.

The new road ran through Gamston and Eaton to Retford, where it linked with the southern end of Carolgate and passed through the town *via* the market place and Bridgegate, over the river Idle, past West Retford Parish Church and then straight on to Barnby Moor. Its beneficial effect upon the town was immediate, particularly for the inns, which now welcomed long-distance travellers. Many new ones were opened and existing inns, such as the White Hart, were quickly enlarged to cope with the extra trade. The old route of the Great North Road quickly fell into disuse; it had always been a poor section and unpopular but Retford's gain spelt financial ruin for places such as the Rushey Inn and the Eel Pie Inn, so named after its reputation for serving the finest eel pie on the Great North Road. The eels came from the nearby river Maun.

Almost before Retford could adjust to its new trade and prosperity news came of an even more important proposal. A group of powerful people, who included the Dukes of Devonshire and of Newcastle, were seeking to build a canal that would run from Chesterfield, through Worksop to Retford and on to either Gainsborough or West Stockwith, where it would make a junction with the river Trent. East Retford Corporation quickly declared its support for the scheme and, at a public meeting held at the Crown in 1770, the new Chesterfield Canal Company decided to apply to Parliament for an enabling Act.

On 29 March 1771 the news reached Retford that Parliamentary approval had been granted and the Corporation immediately ordered that the church bells should be rung for four days. It also made plans to secure a virtual monopoly over the canal as it passed through East Retford, by setting up its own wharf and imposing restrictions that prohibited the opening of any other wharves or warehouses on the waterfront in the town. Putting economic expediency before legal niceties it sold part of the town's common land to the Canal Company and enclosed an area at the southern end of Carolgate as the site of its wharf. The fact that the land in question belonged to the commoners and they were not given the opportunity to object or consent was obviously considered of less importance than the benefits to the town as a whole.

Construction of the canal was begun west of Worksop and the first boats reached West Retford in 1774. The wharf established there was the head of navigation, until the difficult work of raising the embankment and building the three aqueducts required to carry the waterway over the river Idle and its adjoining marshlands had been completed. One of the first cargoes to arrive was of coal and this was sold at l0s 6d (52p) per ton compared to the 15s 6d (77p) for that brought by road.

Between Chesterfield and Retford the canal was built to a narrow beam gauge, which meant that its locks could only pass boats that were no wider than 7 ft but, before the section to West Stockwith was begun, the Canal Company was asked to make it wide enough to be used by boats coming off the Trent. Retford Corporation and several individuals made a contribution towards the extra costs involved, probably still with an eye on the Bawtry trade. The money was spent unnecessarily for there is no record of any wide-beamed boats using the canal.

Retford's Corporation wharf was one of the biggest on the canal and soon became the town's commercial heart and greatest source of income. Several coal, stone, timber and other merchants set up business there and the Corporation gained by renting sites to them and receiving wharfage fees on all the goods handled. Most of the warehouses, workshops and cottages that used to be crowded together on the wharf have long since been demolished, but the original warehouse still stands and is now a popular restaurant.

Early in the canal's history the monopoly enjoyed by the Corporation was successfully challenged and a second wharf opened, to which access was gained by a short arm off the main line near Spa Common. Virtually all traces of this wharf have disappeared beneath a modern builders merchant's yard.

With the Great North Road and the Chesterfield Canal, Retford at last had the good communications that it needed. From the White Hart Hotel, which had become a famous coaching inn, over eighteen stage coaches a day left for places such as Edinburgh, Newcastle and York in the north and London in the south. From the two wharves, regular packet boat services for goods and passengers were operated to Chesterfield, Lincoln, Boston and intermediate places daily, with connections to ships sailing to Hull, London and overseas.

Retford's greater prosperity was reflected in the rebuilding of its houses in the then fashionable Georgian style and in the expansion of the town along Carolgate and around the canal wharf. The canal was finally completed in 1777 and, for the following 67 years, enjoyed an untroubled existence virtually free from competition, at least as far as the carriage of freight was concerned. During that time many of the area's roads were considerably improved under the turnpike trust system and a toll bridge was built at Gainsborough in 1787, but they posed no threat to canal traffic.

The Retford to Worksop road was turnpiked in 1822 and that to Littleborough in 1824, but by 1836 the system was already in decline and extremely unpopular. During November of that year East Retford Borough Council, as a creditor of the Gainsborough to Retford Turnpike Trust, gave its consent to the removal of the toll bar at Moorgate. By 1878 most of the roads in the Retford area had been freed of tolls but already their trade and much of the canal's had been lost to the railways.

News of the first railway to serve Retford was received by the Borough Council in 1844, when it was agreed that 'the proposed railway from Sheffield to Lincoln through Retford would be highly beneficial to this town and neighbourhood and that the Council should use all the means in its power for its support'. Seven months later it also pledged its support for the proposed London to York railway and, in March 1845, petitioned Parliament in favour of the Sheffield and Lincolnshire line. The Duke of Newcastle, as Lord High Steward of the Borough, was requested to present to the House of Lords the Council's petition supporting the Great Northern Railway, and by 1847 negotiations were well advanced to sell land to the railway companies.

The first of the two railways opened for traffic was the Manchester, Sheffield and Lincolnshire on 16 July 1849, with an attractive station at Thrumpton. On 4 September of the same year the Great Northern line was also opened and its trains used the Thrumpton station until 1852, when the present one came into use. Initially this was inconvenient, for it was at least a mile from the town centre and with no direct access road but, within a few months, a connecting loop was made between the two railways, and the Thrumpton station was closed.

A third railway, the Midland, also announced plans to build a line to Retford and its station was to have been on a site close to the town centre. But the plans came to nothing and the nearest that the Midland railway came was at a junction with the MSLR near Worksop, although some Midland trains did arrive at Retford station, pulled by another company's engine.

Both the canal and the railways brought considerable benefits to Retford and without either it could easily have declined to village status, but not everyone stood to gain. The opening of the canal resulted in the closure of most of the district's windmills, as steam-driven roller mills, fed by coal brought by boat, were built on its banks. Railways sounded the death knell for the stage coaches and many of the inns that depended upon them. The Bell at Barnby Moor was one such; it had been one of the premier coaching inns on the Great North Road with as many as 100 horses in its stables at any time but, when the railway came, it had to close.

The White Hart also lost much of its passing trade but its owners adapted to the times and developed its local business. Instead of providing change horses for the Royal Mail and other coaches it conveyed passengers from the town centre to the railway station and met every train. It also acted as the town's parcel office for the Great Northern Railway.

Many new jobs were created at Retford by the railways and they attracted an influx of workers, with a need for more housing. Most of the new building took place in the southern part of East Retford and gradually extended as far as the railway station, making that a part of the town rather than being isolated from it.

Canal-carrying was hit particularly hard by the railways but initially the Chesterfield Canal looked set for a secure future. When news of the proposal to build a railway from Sheffield to Lincoln reached the Chesterfield Canal Company the reaction of its directors was to propose a rival line and thereby force its rivals into take-over talks. Their ploy was successful, the canal was sold to the railway company and all the shareholders were paid out, either in cash or in railway shares. A condition of the sale was that the railway company was required to maintain the canal in a navigable condition and not divert its trade to the trains.

At first the railways company made every effort to improve the condition of the canal and keep up the tonnages carried. In 1882 it even built a new warehouse near Retford town lock during a dispute with the Borough Council over security at the Corporation wharf. But it all came to nothing, as gradually the better services offered by the railways attracted more and more traffic.

Due to its position astride two railways Retford was well served. In 1922 there were nine trains every weekday to London, 14 to Sheffield and equally frequent services to the north and to the east coast. It is a popularly held belief that, if the Great Northern Railway Company had succeeded with its original plans, it would have built its huge engine and carriage works at Retford instead of Doncaster. It is said that East Retford Borough Council considered the matter but decided it was better for the town to stay as it was than be swamped by industrialisation. Since then many people have criticised that decision but, when one considers the problems which arose for Doncaster when the plant works were constructed perhaps the old Council was right. There can be no doubt that, if the Council had welcomed the works, the whole character of Retford would have been irreversibly changed.

There is another, more prosaic, account of why the railway works were located at Doncaster and not Retford, which relates to the availability of land. It seems that the Great Northern Railway considered three possible locations at Peterborough, Retford and Doncaster and of those, only the latter had a site both large enough and geographically ideal.

After losing most of their traffic to the railways, even major routes such as the Great North Road became weed grown and neglected, but all that was to change when motors appeared. At first they were not taken seriously and no one saw them as a threat to the railways. Retford's first garage licensed to sell petrol was that of Charlie Clark who, in 1909, owned one of the five cars registered in the town.

Soon other cars were seen on the town's roads when people such as Sir Joseph Laycock of Wiseton Hall, one of Retford's magistrates, found them preferable to their horse-drawn carriages. None of the roads had been tarmaced and the great clouds of dust thrown up by cars soon became a problem; the Council tried to overcome this by employing men to sprinkle water on the streets. There were worse problems to come as the trickle turned to a flood of vehicles. By 1929 it had become obvious that Retford's narrow roads could not cope with the volume of motor traffic already using the Great North Road, all of which had to squeeze through the confines of Carolgate. In that year the Mayor of East Retford made a public appeal for a by-pass, thus attempting to reverse the decision made 163 years earlier to bring in the traffic of the Great North Road.

By the 1950s Retford, along with towns such as Newark, Grantham and Stamford, had become a notorious bottleneck for traffic travelling north and south. Long tailbacks were a daily occurrence and town life became intolerable as huge lorries inched their way through Bridgegate and Carolgate, often mounting the footpaths to pass each other. To walk along either road was to risk being hit by passing traffic and many accidents occurred. Partial relief came in the 1960s when the Great North Road, known as the A1, was diverted to run between Markham Moor and Blyth. But still the town centre was having to cope with too many vehicles and it was obvious that a ring road would have to be constructed. There was a price to pay, for the chosen route cut through ancient Spa Common and required the demolition of property in Moorgate. Eventually all was completed and the County Council was able to embark upon the pedestrianisation of the town centre, a scheme which would attract much controversy.

During the late 1980s it was the railway that again came to the forefront of Retford's communications, when the main line between Leeds and London was electrified. This brought Retford to within one hour 40 minutes of London and the first commuters began to live in the area. For them the daily journey to London was worthwhile if they and their families could live in the rural surroundings of north Nottinghamshire. The main road from London to the north is now a horrendous ribbon of fast-moving traffic, beset by appalling accidents and delays. It has none of the glamour enjoyed by the old Great North Road in the heydays of stage-coach travel, but fortunately it no longer includes Retford on its route.

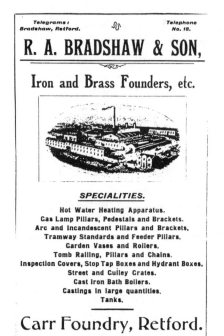

The tomb railings and gas pillars were all made at the Carr Foundry.

The White Hart was a prosperous place when the Dennett family owned it.

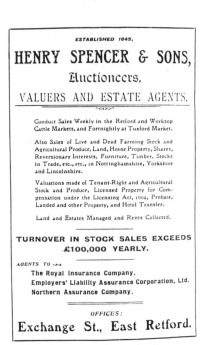

Henry Spencer advertised the cattle markets.

Ye Olde Bell, Barnby Moor — once a Great North Road goldmine.

The Olde Bell, Barnby Moor — back view of the hotel c1905.

	33	34	35	36	37	38	39	40	41	42	43	44	45	46	47	48	49	50	51	52	53	54	55	56	57	58	59	60	61	62	63	64
Elsham.............					5 28					6 15																			9 13			
Barnetby........arr.					5 36					6 23																aft			9 19			
690 London (Mar.)..dep.									1215		aft			aft												3 20						
Sheffield (Victoria)dep.					3 30				4 26	4 25	30			5 40			6 12								7 40						
Darnall, for Hands-					3 36									5 46											7 46						
Woodhouse .....[worth					3 44									5 53											7 53						
Waleswood					3 49									5 59											7 58						
Kiveton Park........					3 58									6 8											8 6						
Shireoaks 727........					4 3									6 14			aft								8 11						
Worksop 671					4 10				4 49	5	6 5	57		6 21			6 37	7 12							8 19						
Checker House.......					4 17									6 29											8 26						
Retford 332, 338..arr.					4 27					5 0	6 8			6 39			6 48	7 23							8 36						
339 PETERBRO' (G.N.)arr.					5 46					6 38						9 24															
339 London (K.C.). "					7 15					8 10				Stop																	
Retford ....dep					4 30													aft							7 35						
Leverton					4 42													7 47													
Cottam					4 47													7 52													
Torksey					4 51													7 56													
Saxilby ....{327, 699					5 0													8 5													
Lincoln (High St.)arr.					5 13				5 45									8 18													
327 NORWICH (Th'p)arr.										9 36							1 58														
288 CROMER (G.E.).. "																															
296 LOWESTOFT (Ch.) "										1028																					
327 YARMOUTH (V.).. "										1034							3 0														
327 IPSWICH .... "										9 3																					
327 HARWICH (Twn) "										9 51																					
327 CAMBRIDGE..... "										8 16							1245														
286 NEWMARKET ... "										9/17																					
332 London (K.C)..arr.										1-50				aft			4 0														
Retford............dep										5 3				5 10			6 51	7 29													
Sturton..........														5 21				7 41													
Gainsborough **327									5 21					5 34			7 30	7 52													
Blyton, for Corringham														5 43				8 1													
Northorpe...........														5 49				8 7													
Kirton Lindsey.......														5 56				8 14													
Scawby and Hibaldstow														6 4				8 22													
Brigg.............										5 44				6 10			7 32	8 28													
Barnetby 699, 708					5 37					6 26				6T30				8 39									9 36					
708 Barnetby * ...arr.														6 43																		
708 Frodingham * ..														7 10																		
708 Thorne *														7 40																		
709 Doncaster * ...arr.														8 6																		
Brocklesby.........					5 45					6 46				6 40													9 45					
715 Hull (Cor. P.)*..arr.										8 0				8 0			1050										1050					
Habrough..........														6 44				8 52									9 49					
Stallingboro'........														6 52				9 0									r					
Healing............														6 55				9 3									r					
Great Coates........														6 58				9 7									r					
Grimsb. Town 363 arr.										6 10				7 3			7 55	9 11									10 3					
Grimsby Docks.... "										6 17				7 12			8 3	9 19									1010					
New Clee .... "										6 52				7 16			8 7															
Cleethorpes........ "										6 57				7 20			8 11	9 25									1016					

MANCHESTER, GORTON, FAIRFIELD, and GUIDE BRIDGE.—Great Central.

The Great Central Railway was busy enough, as this 1900s timetable clearly shows.

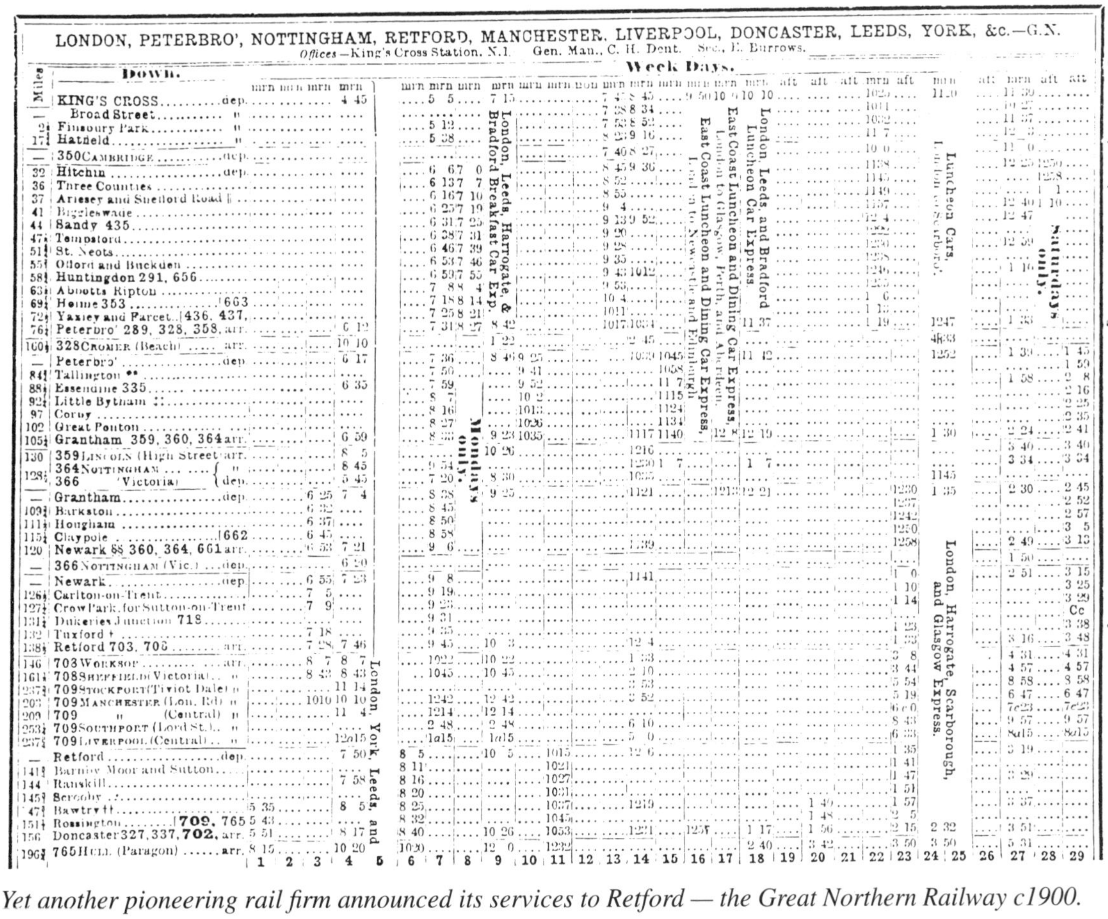
LONDON, PETERBRO', NOTTINGHAM, RETFORD, MANCHESTER, LIVERPOOL, DONCASTER, LEEDS, YORK, &c.—G.N.

Offices—King's Cross Station, N.1. Gen. Man., C. H. Dent. Sec., E. Burrows.

Week Days.

Miles	Down.	1	2	3	4
		mrn	mrn	mrn	mrn
	KING'S CROSS dep.	....	....	....	4 45
—	Broad Street "	....	....	....	....
2½	Finsbury Park "	....	....	....	....
17¾	Hatfield "	....	....	....	....
—	350 Cambridge dep.	....	....	....	....
32	Hitchin dep.	....	....	....	....
36	Three Counties	....	....	....	....
37	Arlesey and Shefford Road ‖	....	....	....	....
41	Biggleswade	....	....	....	....
44	Sandy 435	....	....	....	....
47½	Tempsford	....	....	....	....
51¾	St. Neots	....	....	....	....
55¾	Offord and Buckden	....	....	....	....
58¾	Huntingdon 291, 656	....	....	....	....
63½	Abbotts Ripton	....	....	....	....
69¼	Holme 353, 663	....	....	....	....
72½	Yaxley and Farcet 436, 437,	....	....	....	....
76¼	Peterbro' 289, 328, 358, arr.	....	....	....	6 12
160½	328 Cromer (Beach) arr.	....	....	....	10 10
—	Peterbro' dep.	....	....	....	6 17
84¼	Tallington **	....	....	....	....
88½	Essendine 335	....	....	....	6 35
92¼	Little Bytham ‡‡	....	....	....	....
97	Corby	....	....	....	....
102	Great Ponton	....	....	....	....
105½	Grantham 359, 360, 364 arr.	....	....	....	6 59
130	359 Lincoln (High Street) arr.	....	....	....	8 5
128½	364 Nottingham "	....	....	....	8 45
	366 (Victoria) dep.	....	....	....	5 45
—	Grantham dep.	....	....	6 25	7 4
109¾	Barkston	....	....	6 32	....
111½	Hougham	....	....	6 37	....
115¼	Claypole 662	....	....	6 45	....
120	Newark §§ 360, 364, 661 arr.	....	....	6 53	7 21
—	366 Nottingham (Vic.) dep.	....	....	....	6 20
—	Newark dep.	....	....	6 55	7 23
126½	Carlton-on-Trent	....	....	7 5	....
127½	Crow Park, for Sutton-on-Trent	....	....	7 9	....
131½	Dukeries Junction 718	....	....	....	....
132	Tuxford †	....	....	7 18	....
138¼	Retford 703, 708 arr.	....	....	7 28	7 46
146	703 Worksop arr.	....	....	8 7	8 7
161¼	708 Sheffield (Victoria) "	....	....	8 43	8 43
237¾	709 Stockport (Tiviot Dale) "	....	....	....	11 14
203	709 Manchester (Lon. Rd) "	....	....	1010	10 10
209	709 " (Central) "	....	....	....	11 4
253¼	709 Southport (Lord St.) "	....	....	....	....
237¾	709 Liverpool (Central) "	....	....	....	12a15
—	Retford dep.	....	....	....	7 50
141¾	Barnby Moor and Sutton	....	....	....	....
144	Ranskill	....	....	....	7 58
145¾	Scrooby	....	....	....	....
147¾	Bawtry ††	5 35	....	....	8 5
151¼	Rossington 709, 765	5 43	....	....	....
156	Doncaster 327, 337, 702, arr.	5 51	....	....	8 17
196¾	765 Hull (Paragon) arr.	8 15	....	....	10 20

London, York, Leeds, and ...

London, Leeds, Harrogate, & Bradford Breakfast Car Exp.

Mondays only.

East Coast Luncheon and Dining Car Express.

East Coast Luncheon and Dining Car Express.

London Leeds, and Bradford Luncheon Car Express.

Luncheon Cars.

London, Harrogate, Scarborough, and Glasgow Express.

Saturdays only.

Yet another pioneering rail firm announced its services to Retford — the Great Northern Railway c1900.

JOHN L. PLANT
DRAPER,
TAILOR, HATTER, OUTFITTER,
GENERAL

FURNITURE WAREHOUSE

Bedsteads, Bedding, Chairs,
Perambulators, &c.

MILLINERY & DRESSMAKING
AT MODERATE PRICES BY COMPETENT HANDS.

Full-sized Bedstead from 10/6
CHEAPEST IN THE TRADE.

FURNITURE, &c., supplied on the Hire System.
Easy Payments.

**BLANKETS, SHEETS AND SHEETINGS, FLANNELS,
SHIRTINGS, CALICOES, &c.,**
OF THE BEST QUALITY AT THE LOWEST PRICES.

A VERY LARGE STOCK OF
*Men's, Youths', and Boys' Suits, Trousers, Overcoats,
Scarfs, Collars, Braces, Hats and Caps.*

RETFORD, TUXFORD, & OLLERTON.

Bedsteads started at 10s 6d (52.5p) in 1889.

Lessons at Law

EAST Retford was theoretically ruled by its Corporation from at least 1608 when James I clearly defined the status of the town and the manner in which its Council was appointed. However, the responsibilities which that august body was required to assume were less clear, and cannot be compared to those of local government today. The prime functions of the Corporation were to manage and protect the market, collect tolls at the various bridges which the King had bestowed upon the town, assist the magistrates in keeping law and order and act as the trustee of any property or funds left to the town for charitable purposes.

When it came to matters such as sanitation, maintenance of roads and the care of the sick and needy the Corporation could, if it so wished, ignore the problem and leave it to the Church and private benefactors. In practice, the Corporation did play its part in obtaining social and environmental improvements for residents of the Borough. In comparison to the corporations and guilds of many other towns the Corporation of East Retford was not particularly wealthy. Its income was derived from tolls, market dues and rents from the various properties it owned, out of which it had to maintain the Moot Hall (later known as the Town Hall), pay for the services of various officials such as the town clerk, two sergeants at mace and a town crier, and above all ensure that it conducted the affairs of the town in a style and manner that would enhance its prestige.

Care of the highways and help for the needy was the responsibility of the parish, or church council. This was a body of people that met from time to time in the vestry of the parish church. They would appoint from their number people to carry out duties such as churchwarden, overseer of the poor, surveyor of the highways and the parish constable, for which none of them received any payment. Another post that had to be filled was that of the pindar, whose job was to round up stray cattle and hold them in the parish pinfold, until they were claimed by their owners on payment of a fee or fine. To pay for the services they provided the councils were empowered to levy a rate upon the town's property owners, including the Corporation. In fact several rates were levied, such as a poor rate, a highways rate and a church rate and they were just as unpopular as the council tax is today.

In spite of an apparent indifference by Parliament to the old or infirm much was done locally. In Retford the best-known examples of local concern are Sloswicke's 'hospital' in Churchgate, Trinity Hospital at West Retford and the Corporation almshouses in Union Street. Richard Sloswicke died in 1657 and in his will instructed that, after the death of his wife, his property was to be used to care for six poor elderly men. Things did not work out quite as he intended; after a lawsuit in 1681 the property was transferred to the Corporation. Apart from providing accommodation and a small pension for a few elderly men, not much else happened until 1806, when the old hospital was pulled down and a new one built, consisting of four small houses, with two more added in 1819.

The old building bore an inscription which said 'Mesne de Dieu — ex dono — Richardi Sloswicke Generosi' and this was repeated on the 1806 building but with the words 'Rebuilt 1806 Beaumont Marshall, George Thornton — Gents. Bailiffs'. Perhaps determined not to be outdone, the bailiffs of the time when the rear extension was built also had their names inscribed on a tablet saying 'Erected Anno Domini 1819 — John Parker Esq., John Houst Gent. Bailiffs'. Both tablets can still be seen.

West Retford's Trinity Hospital is to this day one of the area's finest buildings and still provides secure and comfortable homes for elderly men, much as its founder intended. Trinity Hospital was established according to the will of John Darrel, who died in 1665, which directed his executors to convert his former home — West Retford Old Hall — into a hospice for sixteen aged men of good reputation. It was to be known as the Hospice of the Holy and Undivided Trinity in West Retford, and managed by a board of governors. The master governor was to be the Sub-Dean of Lincoln Cathedral and the rector of West Retford the chaplain. A bailiff was to be responsible for the management of the hospice and of its estate and a 'grave, ancient woman' to serve as a nurse.

The inmates were to be known as brothers and were required to observe strict rules such as:

'Every brother is to receive the Sacrament at least three times a year and go to church whenever there is a service there.'

'A brother who is a drunkard, or swearer, or a blasphemer, or an obstinate refuser to go to church will be expelled.'

Each brother received ten shillings (50p) per week (increased to 55p in 1863). They were also given a supply of coal, a cloak and a feast in the common room every Trinity.

When a vacancy occurred, the master governor was to present candidates and, according to John Darrel's will, they must be from the Retford neighbourhood. However, it seems some others were admitted as brethren, for East Retford Borough Council in the 1830s threatened the Sub-Dean of the time with legal action for failing to observe the rule.

By 1828 the Old Hall had become dilapidated and it was decided to rebuild according to the design of Edward Blore, who had been involved in work on several famous buildings, such as Lambeth and Buckingham Palaces. In 1872 further embellishments were added, including a clock tower, and an audit, or dining room, together with a chapel. When it was first established, Trinity Hospital was short of funds and the lands with which it had been endowed produced little income; however, a windfall came when the Chesterfield Canal Company paid £300 for a strip of land. Further financial gains followed as a result of the building of the Great Northern Railway station, when new roads were laid out by the Trinity Hospital trustees, such as Victoria Road, Darrel Road and Cobwell Road. Having built the roads, the trustees then sold the land alongside them as building plots.

The Trinity trustees also completely transformed the West Retford section of Bridgegate which, in 1847, was described as part of the 'miserable village of West Retford' with thatched houses and barns divided from the Borough by a narrow hump-back bridge of five stone arches over the river Idle. The funds to carry out the re-building of Bridgegate were obtained from the sale of land to the railway companies. If you look carefully at most of the properties, you will see on them the initials THT (Trinity Hospital Trustees).

On a far more modest scale than either Sloswicke's or Trinity hospitals are the Corporation almshouses, which are on one side of Union Street. This terrace of nine houses was built in 1825 by the Corporation of East Retford to replace older almshouses that stood along Carolgate and had become dilapidated. They were originally intended to house eighteen poor, elderly women with two in each house, but that was later altered to single occupation. From the sale of the Carolgate site, and with charitable gifts from various donors, the Corporation was able to earn enough interest on the capital to provide two tons of free coal to each house every year, but there was not enough to pay any pensions.

Until the early 1800s, assistance to the poor was confined to 'out relief' which in effect was the doling out of bread and small sums of money by the Overseer of the Poor. To add to this, various people gave money in their wills or by donation — such as Robert Sutton of Kelham who, in 1776, gave to the vicar and churchwardens of East Retford a share in the Chesterfield Canal Company, which was expected to yield an annual dividend of £8 to be distributed among their needy parishioners. In 1812 Ann Woolley left to the Corporation a yearly rent charge on a plot of land to the value of £10. Two thirds of this was to be given to twenty of the oldest and poorest women in the Borough and the rest to the rector of West Retford for ten of the same in his parish. Thomas Welsh in 1818 left £100 to the care of the Corporation out of which they were to distribute £5 yearly among ten poor widows.

On occasions the plight of the poor would touch the hearts of the town's rulers and they would attempt to provide extra relief, such as during a prolonged cold spell in the winter of 1838, when the Council ordered the treasurer to 'pay for a boat load of coal [about 22 tons] to be distributed to the poor of East Retford'.

Most parishes took great care to ensure that they did not find their ratepayers supporting poor people (paupers as they were known) from anywhere else, since each parish had to look after its own. West Retford's accounts of the Overseer of the Poor in 1777 refer to a payment of 7s 7d made to a Mr Buck and Mr Baines for 'going to Sheffield and taking Geo. Shard and getting him married to Ann Fielding who was with child'. No doubt Ann Fielding was supported by the Sheffield ratepayers and had named George Shard as the father of her expected child. So that he could be made to support them, West Retford was told to get them married or make regular maintenance payments, so lost no time in getting him to Sheffield and the pair of them in church before a minister.

Eventually the system of giving outdoor relief, as it was known, was replaced with the equally degrading one of residential workhouses. Many parishes converted buildings for such use and their poor had no option but to move in or receive no help at all. As early as 1744 the two parishes of East and West Retford formed a partnership to establish a workhouse for joint use. In 1818 a union of several parishes in the area was formed and a new workhouse built in Grove Street by the Corporation at a cost of £1,000. The poor of twenty-six surrounding parishes could be sent there, each parish contributing £3 per annum plus three shillings (15p) per week for each person sent.

This was replaced in 1838 by a larger establishment which could house 200 people and was to serve 50 parishes within the Retford Union, formed as a result of the 1834 Poor Law Amendment Act. It stood in what was then open country at the top of Spital Hill. Built of brick, it had three wings radiating from a central block, with exercise yards in between. Administered by a Board of Guardians, with a resident master and a nurse, the Retford workhouse was as unpopular as were all other such establishments. But for many the harsh conditions and rules enforced there were probably better than being destitute outside, for at least they had a roof over their heads and regular meals.

Workhouses had to operate on a shoestring budget and everything possible was done to economise. The inmates who were fit enough had to work for their keep and one of the most hated tasks was that of stone-breaking. The Guardians would have loads of boulder-sized stone delivered to the workhouse, where it was broken down into small pieces to be sold to the parishes or to East Retford Borough Council for road mending.

Over the years the management of the workhouses became more enlightened but they remained detested places. They were not finally abolished until as late as 1948, when Retford Workhouse became known as Hillcrest Hospital and was used as an old people's home. Efforts were made to make the place comfortable and homely but the old atmosphere remained until it was closed and demolished in the 1970s.

Just as the care of the elderly and the poor used to be at a meagre level so too was that of the sick. Retford Hospital at North Road was opened in 1923, having been built as the result of fund-raising and generous gifts, including that of the site. It was served by local doctors and visiting specialists. Enlarged in 1932, it eventually came under the management of the Worksop and Retford Hospital Management Committee, when the National Health Service was set up in 1948.

There was previously a small hospital with a dispensary at Thrumpton Lane which had also been established by charitable donations in 1904. Originally a private house known as White Hall, it was extended several times and gave excellent service to the town until it was superseded by the new hospital. Prior to 1865 there was no provision for the sick in Retford other than that offered by local doctors, who relied upon fees for their living. In that year a dispensary was opened in Chapelgate as a result of a vigorous fund-raising campaign in which Lady Galway of Serlby Hall near Scrooby had been actively involved. Poor people were treated free and medicines were paid for by further fund-raising and in 1887 a cottage hospital was opened alongside the dispensary.

Unfortunately there were no medical facilities to help Retford cope with a succession of plagues. The first known serious outbreak occurred in 1451, when half East Retford's population died. Equally serious was an outbreak of influenza in 1485 which killed hundreds of people, and that was followed in 1558 by a plague which killed over 300 in East Retford and 82 in West Retford. Death came quickly and the churchyards were soon full, causing new burial grounds to be opened.

It was at that time when the legend of the town's two Broad Stones came about. One of the stones is now outside the Town Hall and this is said to have stood at Dominie Cross Roads at the edge of town. During the plague it was the nearest that people from the surrounding countryside would come with their produce, for fear of being infected. The money with which they were paid had to be placed in a bowl of vinegar on the Broad Stone in the belief that any germs would so be killed. Little did they realise that the rats which spread the disease could run unimpeded from the town's broken sewers, along the ditches and dykes, to the equally unsanitary drains of their villages. The base of the second Broad Stone is now in West Retford churchyard, and it too was previously used to hold bowls of vinegar at the town's edge.

When it comes to education, Retford's is a fascinating story. It all revolves around two of the town's former organisations, that of the King Edward VI Grammar School and the Corporation of East Retford. The town nearly lost that school and the Corporation came to the brink of bankruptcy. The saga began in 1551 when Edward VI responded to a petition from the bailiffs and burgesses of East Retford, asking for the establishment of a Free Grammar School for the better education of the youths of the parish. To help finance it, the King endowed it with certain lands which the Crown had gained at the Reformation and East Retford Corporation undertook to make annual payments towards its upkeep. Instead of the school being left to manage its own rent-producing properties, these were vested in the Corporation.

At first all went well, the school was opened in newly built premises on Chapelgate, near to the parish church, and soon the presence of its pupils in the town and as choir boys at church services became an established feature of everyday life. Unfortunately, in 1651 the town was struck by a severe storm, which brought down the church tower and the Corporation sold property to pay for the repairs. Some of the property sold did not in fact belong to the Corporation, but was part of that held in trust for the Grammar School. No one seemed to be aware of this or, if they were, thought it did not matter, because the Corporation was still paying the schoolmaster's salary.

Trouble came in 1699 when the then schoolmaster proved that the value of the estates vested in the Corporation should have produced an annual income of £145, instead of the £29 a year which the school had received. The matter was taken to Court and the Corporation was ordered to pay the schoolmaster the sum of £3,372 plus £60 costs. As one would expect, the Corporation was not happy about this and appealed, saying that the schoolmaster ought to consider himself lucky to be paid £30 a year over and above what he made by teaching fee-paying boys. They also pointed out that they had built the schoolhouse at a cost of £300 and kept it in repair. The Corporation won its appeal and the matter appeared settled.

In 1827 another headmaster tried again and a Commission of Enquiry was set up; the response of the Corporation was to stop paying his salary. The case against the Corporation was taken to the Law Lords, who found in favour of the school, but again the Corporation appealed and prevaricated. At the reform of local government in 1835 the Corporation was itself abolished and one of the first resolutions made by the new East Retford Borough Council was to seek a speedy settlement of the School Chancery suit. Still the wrangling continued until, in 1847, the Council was ordered to pay into Court the sum of £2,753, the value of the alienated lands. The Council did not possess that much money and had to sell or mortgage most of its property to raise it. This in turn reduced its income, leaving insufficient funds to pay outstanding accounts, and the Council had to borrow to pay its creditors.

The school guardians decided to use the money to help build a new school and, in spite of past differences, the Borough Council helped find the site on London Road where the present building stands. Work began in 1853 to build a school with classrooms for 120 boys, accommodation for 20 boarders and a master's house. Further accommodation was added in later years and in 1937 the present assembly room with its stage was erected, to provide the setting for many concerts, prizegivings and speech days.

Important as the grammar school was to the town it only taught a small percentage of the children; many more went to schools initially set up by the churches. The National Schools movement, which was the name given to a country-wide society formed to provide elementary education to all children, opened a school in Grove Street during 1858, replacing an earlier one in Chapelgate provided by the parish church. In 1876 it became compulsory for all children, to attend school until they reached the age of ten, and to enforce this, local school boards were set up and attendance officers employed. Later developments included the establishment of the prestigious Girls' High School, a teacher training unit at the Grammar School and a further National School at West Retford. Although only a small town, Retford was educationally well served and its schools held in high repute.

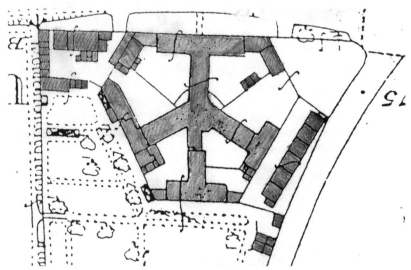

The Spital Hill Workhouse was built by the East Retford Union in 1838 — this is the plan, and the only extant illustration of what it was like.

Sloswicke's Hospital was rebuilt in 1806.

Trinity Hospital — the 1872 building.

Retford Grammar School — an old print.

The County High School soon after completion.

The former Dispensary and Cottage Hospital on Chapelgate first opened in 1865.

Cottage Hospital, Whitehall. 1913.

The former Wesleyan School at Grove Street.

Telephone 88.

Corporation Wharf, Retford, *llllar* 192 8

Mr Collon

Dr. to G. HURST & SON,

TIMBER AND BUILDERS' MERCHANTS.

Dealers in all kinds of Wheelwrights' Timber.

Slates, Ridging, Chimney Pots, Sanitary Pipes, Gulley Traps for Sinks, Fire
Bricks, Roofing Felt, Staffordshire Blue Building, Stable, Causeway, Channel
Bricks, and Wall Copings, Oak, Elm, Chestnut, and Pitchpine Coffin Boards,
Plaster Cement, Lime, Roofing and Glass Tiles, Tile Laths, and Plaster Laths

SHEET AND PLATE GLASS AND SHEET LEAD CUT TO SIZES.

A c's rendered Quarterly. 5 interest charged on a/c's of over 6 month's standing.

Saw Mills : CAROLGATE BRIDGE.

10.0

A bill for 10s (50p) from G. Hurst & Son.

An invitation to visit Clark's works.

*Style and comfort were the hallmarks of the
Northern Rubber Co.*

An early letterheading from E. Swannack & Sons.

21, BRIDGEGATE,
(NEXT THE BRIDGE).
RETFORD. *X̶ ly ꝓ* 191.

jⁿ̃o a↙Moᴠ

DR. TO C. SWANNACK & SON

JOINERS, BUILDERS, CABINET MAKERS, UNDERTAKERS, GENERAL HOUSE FURNISHERS, REMOVERS & STORERS

A large assortment of new & second-hand Furniture, Bedsteads, Bedding, Chairs, Tables

7 Kitchen chairs & &c.   1 14 9
1 more   15 6
                   2 9 3

Furniture from C. Swannack & Son.

J. J. POWELL,

Ladies', Gentlemen's, & Boys'

TAILOR;

16, CAROLGATE, RETFORD.

PROFESSOR TROUSERS & BREECHES
CUTTER.

£3 10s. { Beautiful Suit of plain Black or Worsted, to order.

£2 5s. { Neat Evening or Business Suit, to order.

CUT—EASY-FITTING & STYLISH.

J. J. POWELL'S SPECIALITIES :—

GENTLEMEN'S	LADIES'
Riding Trousers	Jackets
Hunting Breeches	Mantles
Pantaloons	Cloaks
Liveries, &c.	Ulsters
Gentlemen's Tweed Suits, from 42/-	Riding Habits, &c.
Youths' ditto, from 30/-	Ladies' Jackets and Ulsters, from 25/-

MADE TO MEASURE.

J. J. P. is specially desirous that Ladies should honour his Establishment with an early visit, feeling persuaded that his representations will meet with confirmation, and that one trial will ensure to him hereafter a continuance of the patronage he is anxious to obtain.

A suit for £2 5s (£2.25) from J.J. Powell in 1889.

Mangles and lawn mowers from John Curtis.

An undated bank slip of Beckett & Co, Retford — generally known as Foljambe's Bank.

A cheque drawn on the Grove Estate account.

William Battie Wrightson of Cusworth Hall, Doncaster, was one of the contenders in the notorious Parliamentary election of 1826.

First Past the Poll

BECAUSE Retford has never featured in any major upheavals in English history, no epic battles were fought here and kings, bishops and those seeking power passed it by, it is easy to assume that this ancient town has never played a key role in any major drama or excitement. Even the Civil War left everyday life in the town relatively undisturbed, although the frequent passing of rival troops must have caused problems, especially when Charles I travelled through on his way to Newark Castle in 1645. Many years later, during the Jacobite rebellion of 1745, troops used the parish church as an overnight stable.

However, when general elections were held, Retford would come alive and the way that polling was conducted was to earn it the dubious reputation of a 'rotten' borough. Such practices eventually led to the great Reform Act of 1832.

East Retford first began sending representatives to Parliament as early as 1315, but this ceased after fifteen years because of the cost. Nearly 250 years were to pass before the voice of Retford was again heard in the Commons, when the town resumed its right to elect two members. However, due to the electoral system which then operated, the members for East Retford only spoke for about one in twenty-four of its residents as the right to vote was limited. Before the Reform Acts East Retford was a 'freeman' borough, which meant that only those who had been accepted by the Corporation as legitimate freemen could vote at elections. The orthodox way to become a freeman of East Retford was by birthright or by servitude and, as late as 1839, the following entries were made in the records of the Borough Council:

'Swearing in of burgesses:

'By Birthright. William Brown, eldest son of William and Sarah Brown was admitted to the Freedom of the Borough and sworn in as a Burgess.

'By Servitude. Samuel Littlewood, who on the 17th March 1826 was bound apprenticed for the term of 7 years to William Jackson a Burgess of the Borough and on the 16th December 1826 was assigned to John Banks, also a Burgess of this Borough, for the remainder of the term of 7 years, was this day admitted to the Freedom of the Borough and sworn in as a Burgess.'

Small boroughs like East Retford were extremely vulnerable to pressure from wealthy and influential people such as the Dukes of Newcastle. From 1666 to 1865 members of that family held the title of Lord High Steward of East Retford, they owned vast estates nearby and, in return for a person's political support, could help him obtain lucrative employment or trade. Until the passing of the Secret Ballot Act of 1872 those eligible to vote had to do so before the local magistrates and lists of how the votes were cast were put on public display.

The Corporation itself was for many years firmly in the grip of the Newcastle faction and, as it had the power to create freemen, it could do much to influence election results. In 1797, after the Newcastle candidates had been successfully opposed by Sir Wharton Amcotts and William Petrie, the Corporation was fearful that it would suffer a similar defeat and therefore swore in thirty-eight carefully chosen honorary freemen. But this action was challenged in court and ruled to be illegal, the honorary freemen were all ousted, and so were five of the aldermen. As many of those who were aldermen were traders who supplied the surrounding ducal estates, it is hardly surprising that they wished to be seen as supporters.

It was the 1826 election and the subsequent Parliamentary enquiry into the manner in which it had been conducted that earned for East Retford the dubious title of 'rotten borough', and a reputation for electoral corruption. To this day any student of English Parliamentary history will find copious references to East Retford for the Reform Act period. Yet, however much local elections may have warranted accusations of corruption it is wrong to assume that East Retford stood alone or, indeed, was the worst example.

Corruption in many forms was widely practised at elections throughout the country prior to the Reform Acts and the introduction of the secret ballot. At the time of the petition to disenfranchise East Retford, similar moves were made in respect of many other places and, when the 1832 Reform Act was passed, it affected some 90 so called 'rotten boroughs'.

At East Retford, out of a population of nearly 2,500 only about 220 were freemen, with the right to vote, and about half of those lived outside the borough. The 'servitude' qualification, gained by serving a seven years' apprenticeship with a freeman, had resulted in a high proportion of tradesmen holding the balance of power to the exclusion of professional people such as lawyers, bankers and others. People such as Richard Hannam, a lawyer practising in Retford and holding the post of Clerk to the Magistrates, did not have the right. Neither did Francis Thornagh Foljambe, a partner in Retford's first bank and member of the family of that name whose seat was at nearby Osberton. It is understandable that such people resented the power of the freemen and were suspicious of the influence which those such as the Duke of Newcastle could bring to bear upon them.

This division in the town led to the setting up of an independent party, which put up candidates in opposition to those of the Newcastle faction. In turn this was to result in the increase of bribery and manipulation of the voters. When in 1765 the then Duke of Newcastle quarrelled with his two nephews, Lord Lincoln and John Shelley, the rival factions became even more divided and, in the election of 1768, the Duke's expenses came to over £900, mostly spent on bribing and 'treating' the freemen. This expenditure was obviously matched by the rival faction because, in the 1796 election, both seats were won by the Independents and the Duke lost control. It was later proved that the then going rate per vote paid was up to 20 guineas (1 gn = 105p).

In 1812 the Duke of Newcastle attempted to regain his hold on the town; he put up a candidate but then withdrew him, due to the high costs of electioneering. The Independents, led by the Foljambe faction, invited Lord Fitzwilliam, a leading Whig, to put up his candidate, but this was resented by many freemen, who considered the Foljambe influence on the Corporation was now too powerful. They formed what became known as the Blues Club, which held meetings at the Turks Head and had the support of many wealthy townsfolk. The election of 1826 was to become a trial of strength between the two factions, and the cause of scenes such as East Retford had rarely seen before. It was also the last election at East Retford as a Parliamentary Borough.

This was to be a 'no holds barred' election in which bribery, drunkenness, violence and even religion were to play their part. The Foljambe group (nominally Independents but Whig supporters) put up as their candidates Sir Robert Dundas and William Battie Wrightson of Cusworth Hall, near Doncaster. Standing for the Blues was Sir Henry Wright Wilson, a well-known opponent of Catholic emancipation. As was the custom, pre-election dinners were held by the candidates at the town's leading inns, to which freemen were invited. These dinners gave the opportunity for the candidates to make speeches but, more important, for their agents to mingle with freemen and obtain promises of votes in return for the 'usual considerations'. This was the start of the treating of voters to free food and drink that continued up to election day.

Election fever would grip the town, fanned by powerful speeches made from the Broadstone in the Square, the distribution of pamphlets to those who could read, marching bands hired by the rival groups and ever more free beer. The Blues brought in a fiery Protestant clergyman known as Parson Brooks, who made many open-air speeches, in which he warned the freemen that, if they voted for either Dundas or Battie-Wrightson, they would meet with hell's fire and damnation as both were Catholic sympathizers who would bring back Popery. He even mentioned burning at the stake and the Inquisition torture methods. Battie-Wrightson was a quieter, more subtle personality but Dundas, a Major General in the army and a nephew of Lord Fitzwilliam, was a more forceful character.

Each side had its favourite public houses where voters could usually be sure of a free drink. The Blues would frequent the Newcastle Arms, Half Moon, Marquis of Granby and the Turks Head. They would form themselves into parades led by a band playing God Save the King, and a man holding aloft a fox's tail fastened to a long pole. Wearing the party ribbons and waving flags they would march around the town and, if any of their rivals had the misfortune to meet up with them, violence would erupt. The Whigs used the Crown as their headquarters, which was of dubious benefit for its proprietor, who had to regularly contend with having his windows smashed by unruly mobs and, on one occasion, saw his furniture dragged outside and burnt. Once, when Dundas and Battie-Wrightson were at the hotel, a mob of Blues supporters smashed the doors down and broke windows and shutters to get inside. Other Whig inns were the Vine, Mermaid, Angel and Swan.

Perhaps less rowdy was the outing to Cusworth Hall given to some thirty freemen by William Battie-Wrightson. Boarding horse-drawn carriages, they were taken the eighteen miles to Cusworth, where they were treated to a day's hare coursing in the Park, before going to the Red Lion in Doncaster for a dinner and as much as they could drink. Staying overnight they returned to Retford after lunch the following day to continue the party at the Vine. All the costs were paid by Battie Wrightson.

As election day drew closer it became clear that the situation was getting out of hand and, to help keep order, 200 special constables were sworn in, some brought from as far as Sheffield. This displeased Sir William Wright Wilson and led to a confrontation between his supporters and the constables in the churchyard of St Swithun's, at which he is reputed to have said 'Do not insult us, I only have to lift my finger and you will be torn to pieces'. Several of the special constables left for home before election day as a result of being assaulted. Concern over what the mob might do next prompted the Senior Bailiff of the Corporation to request the presence of the Army, and a detachment of Horse Guards was stationed outside the town.

Voting in the 1826 election commenced at 11 am on 9 June amid scenes of great rowdiness; many were already drunk and had come armed with cudgels and various agricultural implements. A great crowd of Blues supporters gathered outside the Town Hall, making it both difficult and dangerous for the Whigs to get into the building. Inside, however, the situation was reversed, for here a solid pack of Whigs threatened any opponent who had the temerity to try to reach the magistrates to declare his vote. There were no polling booths and no secrecy, for freemen had to listen for their names to be called by the Returning Officer and then shout out their votes.

Polling stopped for the day at 4.00pm, and already it was clear that Dundas and Battie-Wrightson had won. This prompted them to make their way through the crowd to the centre of the Square, where they attempted to make speeches. This enraged the mob and, to make matters worse, Dundas stuck his tongue out at them; they were both attacked, Battie-Wrightson, now with two black eyes, managed to escape, while Dundas, helped by constables, had to run for his life to Foljambe Bank (next to the present Town Hall). On the way his coat was torn from his back and many blows aimed at him. The mob then attacked the bank, smashing its windows and attempting to break down the door, until they were confronted by Francis Foljambe brandishing loaded pistols.

At this point the red-coated Horse Guards rode into the Square, headed by the Senior Bailiff of East Retford Corporation, Alderman George Hudson, who began to read the Riot Act but, as he was known to be a leading Whig supporter, the crowd began throwing missiles and he fell from his horse, struck on the head by a stone. The Horse Guards then charged into the crowd, striking out with the flat of their swords; mercifully there were few injuries, only one man losing a thumb and a woman suffering a crushed thigh. It was feared that a man found lying on the ground had been killed but then it was realised he was only dead drunk. Perhaps the most aggrieved were the members of the Blues band; hired to play throughout the election they had been manfully playing God Save the King when the Horse Guards charged them and later claimed they had been egging on the mob.

Throughout the night troops patrolled the town and, before polling was due to begin 'on the second day (it took two days to record 120 votes), Wilson decided to withdraw, and Dundas and Battie-Wrightson were declared duly elected. Outraged by his defeat Sir Henry Wright Wilson appealed to Parliament, saying that the election should be declared void because of the riotous manner in which it had been conducted. A Parliamentary enquiry was held the following May and the Select Committee reported, 'We consider it our duty to direct the serious attention of the House to the corrupt state of the Borough of East Retford. It appears from the evidence of several witnesses that at elections to Parliament for this Borough it has been a long continued, notorious and general practice for the electors who voted for the successful candidates to receive the sum of 20gns [£21] from each of them; so that those who voted for both the returned members got 40gns [£42].' William Battie-Wrightson and Sir Robert Dundas were declared not elected and the election to be void. Both were found guilty of 'treating'.

The events of the 1826 election gave added momentum to the local campaign for reform and were welcomed by those seeking the re-organisation of the electoral system. By 1830 a Bill was before Parliament entitled 'An Act to prevent Bribery and Corruption in the Election of Burgesses to serve in Parliament for the Borough of East Retford'. Witnesses were called by supporters and opponents and all the details of the enquiry recorded and published. Various Retford people found themselves staying in London for several days as a result of signing petitions which both sides had circulated throughout the town.

Leading the Retford supporters was Richard Hannam, a solicitor in the town and a resident for thirty-five years. He had acted as law agent for one of the candidates in the 1812 election and produced evidence of bribery that occurred then. His clerk, William Newton, acted unpaid for a committee that had been formed in the town to end the freemen-only vote and get the franchise extended. That committee became known as the Birmingham Club, as a result of moves to transfer the Retford Parliamentary seats to that town. There were many in Retford who were not bothered what happened as long as the age-old 'freeman' system was abolished, and with it the bribery and corruption. They believed the town would be purer without it.

John Mee, another solicitor and the Town Clerk of East Retford, also supported the Bill, although he was able to prove that, in the 1826 election, the Corporation had not sought to influence the result, even though most of the aldermen had favoured Sir Henry Wright Wilson because he had the tacit, though not openly stated support of the Duke of Newcastle. He also proved that the election had been conducted within the rules that applied at the time and that no new freemen had been created other than by birthright or servitude entitlement.

Those opposed to the Bill included several of the freemen, who set out to deny that they had accepted payment for their votes but, under cross examination, admitted that after an election a 'packet' was usually delivered to their homes at about midnight, although they never saw who brought it. It was clearly established that the 'packets' contained twenty guineas and the messenger was often the Town Crier. That would have been one of the many extra jobs which he would undertake, to supplement the meagre annual salary paid by the Corporation.

There were several terms used in East Retford to avoid mentioning payment for votes. A candidate who had made clear his intention to pay those who had voted for him was known as a Friend, and To Do What Was Right was to pay the 20 guineas. To be Marshed was to fail to get paid, which arose after a candidate named Marsh left town without paying; to Lose An Election meant that you had either not voted or had backed a losing candidate.

Some of the witnesses stuck to their guns and tried to claim that they had no knowledge of bribery, but the lists of those who had been paid were produced at the hearing. Fortunately at the outset all the witnesses called had been guaranteed immunity from prosecution. One witness caused amusement when he said that he had noticed that his wife was always flush with money soon after an election but he claimed not to know why. Presumably she found the mysterious packet before he did. Alderman George Hudson, who was the Corporation's Senior Bailiff and the returning officer at the 1826 election (when he was hit on the head by a stone while attempting to read the Riot Act), denied ever promising his vote but admitted to having received packets.

Francis Foljambe and his chief bank clerk were both given a particularly tough cross examination, but they blamed all the trouble on the 'Blues', claiming that, until Sir Henry Wright Wilson came, the town had been quiet and orderly but from then on 'some of the freemen were drunk for weeks and the town was the scene of riot and confusion which had all been very disgraceful'.

After hearings in both Houses of Parliament the Bill passed its second reading and in 1830 the right to vote was extended to what was known as the 40 shilling freeholders throughout the Hundred of Bassetlaw. They were numerous enough to completely outvote the freemen of the town at the subsequent election and thus ended the delivery of those mysterious packets. However, it was not until the secret ballot was made law in 1872 that coercion by landlords, employers and those who could bestow trade or favours upon those who 'accepted their advice' at election times, was rendered impossible.

Without doubt there was bribery and corruption in the old Borough of East Retford at elections but there is a danger that in more modern times it can be seen out of its true context. What happened there was common practice throughout the country and the payment for a vote was seen by the freemen as a welcome 'perk', just as today people happily accept company cars and expense accounts and try to avoid paying income tax. And how many people could in all honesty claim that, if they were promised the equivalent of a year's salary just for voting for a particular candidate, they would refuse? It was unfortunate for Retford's reputation that its worst election troubles occurred at a time when many people wanted to see reforms carried out, and the happenings in the town during 1826 gave them valuable ammunition.

The Old Bank in The Square — formerly Beckett's (Foljambe's) Bank.

The Newcastle Arms, Bridgegate, scene of many an election crowd.

Celebrations for the coronation of King George V, 1911.

The crest of East Retford Borough.

From Freemen to Freedom

THE freemen of East Retford had hardly recovered from the shock of losing their exclusive right to elect two Members of Parliament, and the cash windfall that every election could bring, when a further loss of power was meted out in 1835. Those that had campaigned for Parliamentary reform were equally determined to see the replacement of the old freeman-appointed Corporations, with local councils elected by a majority of the residents.

To meet the demands of the campaigners, the Government appointed Commissioners to examine the old Corporations, to find out how effective they were in providing services to the towns they controlled. At Retford the Commissioners found that few of the residents had any confidence in the Corporation or respect for it. In their report they said, 'East Retford Corporation is self chosen from a clan not only inferior in station and intelligence but also branded with infamy or long continued and notorious bribery.'

The outcome was an Act of Parliament which abolished the old corporations and the setting up of borough councils in their place. While the measure was considered by Lords and Commons East Retford Corporation sent their Junior Bailiff and the Town Clerk to present a petition in opposition, but to no avail, for the Act received the Royal Assent in 1835. Included was the provision for every male ratepayer in the Borough to have the right to vote, and this effectively brought to an end control by freemen.

One of the last known acts of the old Corporation was to appoint two watchmen to police the town, the one on night duty to be paid 12 shillings (60p) per week and the one on day shift 6s (30p). They were to work seven days a week and alternate shifts in rotation. So began the police force, but for the Corporation it was a case of too little and too late.

On December 1835 a public court, or meeting as we would call it, was held in the Town Hall and presided over by the Senior Bailiff, Joshua Cottam. The purpose of the meeting was to elect twelve councillors 'according to the Act to provide for the regulation of Municipal Corporations in England and Wales'. Just how the election was carried out is not known but, in the absence of a secret ballot, it is doubtful if democracy as we know it was observed. The most votes cast were 156 for Joshua Cottam, described as a gentleman and living in Carolgate. The other elected councillors and the voting figures were:

147	votes	for	William Mee of Bridgegate	Surgeon.
146	"	"	Job Bullivant of Carolgate.	Draper.
132	"	"	John Hudson of the Square.	Wine merchant.
131	"	"	John Mee of Churchgate.	Solicitor.
130	"	"	Edward Parker of Carolgate.	Coal merchant.
120	"	"	William Fisher of Grove Street.	Gentleman.
118	"	"	Gervase King Holmes of the Square.	Solicitor.
113	"	"	Richard Oates of the Square.	Ironmonger.
105	"	"	John Dawber of Carolgate.	Plumber.
103	"	"	John Smith of the Square.	Gentleman.
97	"	"	Thomas Bailey of Bridgegate.	Saddler.

The names of other people who may have stood unsuccessfully were not recorded. The returning officer was Joshua Cottam, so he supervised his own election.

At the first meeting of the elected councillors they in turn elected the four aldermen which the Act required to complete the Council. They were Thomas Bailey, William Dennett, Thomas Hodgkinson and John Parker; their occupations and addresses are not in the minute book, but William Dennett was the well-known proprietor of the White Hart Hotel. How these people were selected is also unrecorded.

On the first day of January 1836 the new Council held its first proper meeting and Gervase King Holmes was elected Mayor. John Cottam was appointed Treasurer and William Newton Town Clerk, both having held those positions with the old Corporation, so there was no lack of continuity. A committee of councillors was set up to examine the general state of the Corporations' finances, establish the sum required to settle the long outstanding Grammar School lawsuit, and to look at all the junior appointments made by the old Corporation to see if they were really necessary. The Treasurer and the Town Clerk were instructed to produce all the accounts and documents belonging to the Council to the committee for examination.

Unlike those of the old Corporation, the minute books of the new East Retford Borough Council have been preserved, and it is fascinating to follow, through their hand-written pages, the story of how the town shook off the inertia of the past and moved into a new era.

One of the prime movers was the Town Clerk, William Newton. He was first appointed by the Corporation in 1832 and continued in office for 44 years. A practising solicitor in the town, he did not work solely for the Council and was merely paid a retaining fee. His influence would have been considerable and that is reflected in the agenda items which he listed for councillors to debate.

Within two months of being formed, the new Council was considering matters which the Corporation would have looked upon as sacrosanct. Among them were items such as:

'To determine whether the salary now paid to the organist of East Retford parish church by the Council should be continued.

'Whether the pews now rented in St Saviour's church be retained.

'Whether the corporation pews in East Retford parish church occupied by the corporation be sold.

'Whether the corporation pews in West Retford parish church be sold.' The organist lost his salary and only the pews in the church at East Retford were kept.

More important matters were set in progress, such as the provision of a proper drainage system, street lighting by gas and the building of a more efficient prison and police office. Two other items discussed at that meeting must have made the members of the former Corporation recoil in horror. The Council was asked to determine whether:

'The maces, cups, punch bowls and other paraphernalia of the corporation be sold.

'How the wines and spirits belonging to the corporation be disposed of.'

Fortunately for Retford they decided to keep the maces and other civic items; in fact, they were augmented over the succeeding years and are still in the possession of the town. They did, however, sell the decanters and glasses, which is a pity, but kept for special occasions the wines and spirits. The use of the word 'paraphernalia' by the Town Clerk indicates his attitude towards any show of civic pomp. However, the standing of the Council in the eyes of residents was raised by admitting ratepayers to its meetings, publishing annual accounts and requiring tenants to come to the Town Hall on a set day each month to pay their rents publicly to the Treasurer.

It was the provision of gas street lighting which was to have the most effect and lead to the expansion of the Borough and the start of municipal enterprise. A private company had set up a gas works along Grove Street in 1831 and, by 1848, was supplying nearly 500 customers. Disputes between it and the Council began in 1863, when the assessment for rates was increased from £110 to £300, just after the Council had demanded, and was given, a reduction in the cost of lighting the street lamps. The arrangements for street lighting were amusing, to say the least, and led to many complaints from the public. There were 76 street lamps and they were supposed to be lit for 2,000 hours between September and April; to save gas they were left off for three nights every four weeks when there was a full moon. So on those nights the lamplighter and his young assistant stayed at home and, if it happened to be cloudy, the town stayed in darkness.

Many were the complaints made about those dark nights, and the Council always blamed the gas company, which peeved the directors, who produced figures showing that they made a loss on street lighting and claimed that they were generous in providing free gas to light up the Town Hall clock. The Council was convinced that it could run the gas works more efficiently and provide cheaper gas to everyone, which led to proposals to buy out the gas company and, as many of its directors were also Councillors, the suggestion was welcomed. The purchase price was £30,000 and, at a public meeting called by the Council in 1876, it was given the backing of ratepayers.

To raise the money the Council applied to the Government's Public Works Commissioners for a loan, claiming that 'the gas works ought to be public property in the hands of the representatives of the ratepayers and for the purpose of providing a supply of better gas at a reasonable price'. This was refused on the grounds that the annual rate yield of the Borough was insufficient to cover the loan. To overcome that, the Council invited deputations from the surrounding parishes to discuss changing the Borough boundaries.

The outcome was the promotion of a Parliamentary bill to incorporate West Retford, Ordsall and Clarborough. At first this was opposed by the Manchester, Sheffield and Lincolnshire Railway Company and by the Great Northern Railway Company, who claimed that it would lead to large increases in rates and charges and that the purchase price for the gas works was excessive; they were only worth £26,000. However, after the MS&LR withdrew its opposition, the GNR followed, and the 'Act for the extension of the boundaries of the Borough of East Retford to enable the Council to acquire the undertaking of the Retford Gas and Coke Company and for other purposes' was passed in July 1878.

West Retford had previously managed its affairs by having a local board, and part of its duties was to administer the various properties that belonged to the parish. These included a row of five cottages that stood opposite the parish school and were let to tenants such as Widow Golland and Widow Barthorpe at annual rents of £4. Because the West Retford properties were transferred to the Borough Council, the Expansion Act required a reduction in the rates charged to West Retford people proportionate to their annual value.

Ordsall parish, however, was in debt. It owed £597 plus interest to the Retford and District Highways Board and the Borough Council had to assume responsibility for payment. Also included in the Act was the authority to acquire the Retford Cattle Market Company for £3,000, but it appears that this was never carried out.

The formal purchase of the Gas Company was completed in 1879 and, under the Borough Councils' management, the works were rapidly expanded. More important for the consumers, the price of gas fell from 3s 4d (17p) per 1,000 cubic feet in 1879 to 2s 6d (12p) in 1904. But gas was not the only matter to occupy the Council at that time; another item of equal importance concerned the town's water supply. In 1879 this came from private wells, the canal and the river Idle; there was a public pump in the Market Place that gave good water and another at Thrumpton. However, this drew water from the Idle and, because it was downstream of the drains, its supply was foul and badly discoloured. An inspector's report of 1876 said that at Moorgate there were 154 houses with a water supply unfit to drink. At Canal Row the two pumps meant to supply 40 houses were out of order but that was perhaps a good thing, as the water they gave was also not fit to drink. The residents carried their water from the canal, which was about 100 yards away.

When a private concern, known as the Retford Water Works Company, applied to the Council for permission to open up the roads, so as to lay water mains, the response was a firm refusal. The Company then applied to Parliament for an enabling Act, but this was strenuously opposed by the Council, who declared that they could do the job cheaper and, as no dividends would have to be paid out of the profits to any sharcholders, the residents would get cheaper water. This was the age of municipal enterprise, encouraged by the Government, so East Retford Borough Council won the argument and was allowed to borrow £15,000 to set up the waterworks. This meant that the Council now operated two of the basic services used by the town.

Although the actions of the Borough Council regarding gas and water met with the approval of most ratepayers, their decision to demolish the old Town Hall and replace it with a new building on the south side of the Square provoked a storm of protest. The objectors were not, as would happen nowadays, against the destruction of the fine Georgian Town Hall but opposed to the expenditure to be incurred in building the new one. They even went so far as presenting a petition to the Lords of the Treasury against the spending of corporate funds at a time when the town still lacked an efficient drainage system and much of its housing was sub-standard.

A counter petition submitted by the Council won the day and permission was given to raise the £9,000 needed by mortgaging the property it owned. This enabled the Council to proceed with its resolution of March 1864 which claimed 'That it would conduce greatly to the general accommodation and work out a striking improvement to the Town if the present Town Hall were to be taken down and one of more commodious and convenient size erected on a site to be provided for that purpose and that Butter, Corn and Meat markets be provided in annexes therewith'. Advertisements were placed in various newspapers inviting architects to submit designs and, out of 18 received, that of Bellamy and Hardy of Lincoln was chosen. They were also the architects of Grimsby and Ipswich town halls and their similarity to that of Retford is noticeable.

It was a major scheme for such a small town and involved the demolition of some existing houses, the creation of a new road (Exchange Street) and the construction, not only of a town hall, but of buildings to house a corn exchange and a meat market. However, with all the confidence of the Victorian era, the councillors pressed on and involved themselves in every detail. Thomas Hopkinson, a builder of

East Retford, won the construction contract, having quoted the price of £6,421 8s 3d (£6421.41) and the foundation stone was laid with due ceremony by the Mayor on 19 June 1866, accompanied by the ringing of the church bells.

Once the scheme got under way, opposition seems to have faded and was replaced by offers of help. The person who had lent the required capital to the Council offered to donate a stained glass window, and a deputation from the town asked for permission to pay for the mechanism needed to make the clock chime the quarters, when it was moved from the old town hall to the new one. They would also buy the extra bells needed, provide the floor in the clock tower and pay all related costs. A gift of a writing case for use in the Mayor's parlour was made by Messrs Mee, Burnaby and Denman.

Eventually the work was completed and the opening ceremonies could take place. On 25 January 1868 a grand ball and dinner was held in the new and opulent Town Hall, with its glittering chandeliers, oil paintings, carpets and atmosphere of civic pride. High up in the ballroom, where nobody could fail to see it, was displayed the crest of the Borough of East Retford. In the butter market hall below the ballroom, a tea party was held for the townspeople's wives and for Sunday school children, which was paid for by the Councillors (except one who refused a contribution). The new council chamber, with its Mayor's parlour, ornate gilt chandeliers (two of which had been brought from the old town hall) and oak furniture, provided a formal setting for meetings of the Council.

Compared with the record of the old Corporation, the achievements of the Borough Council during the first fifty years of its existence were remarkable. They included such items as building a new bridge over the river Idle at Bridgegate, buying out the gas works, providing the town with a piped water supply, building a new town hall, extending the Borough and the setting up of a Board of Health to improve sanitation and living conditions. It even tackled environmental matters, such as smoke emissions from factory chimneys. If the portraits of the Mayors of those days which now hang in the Town Hall make them look austere but confident, it is with good reason.

1. THE Borough of East Retford is co-extensive with the Parish of that name.   ANCIENT LIMITS OF THE BOROUGH.

2. On the North-east the Hamlets of Moorgate and Spittal Hill may be considered as forming part of the Town, the houses being built in continuation of the streets in East Retford. To the South of the Town, immediately after crossing the Chesterfield Canal, is the Township of Little Gringley, in which is situated South Retford, and Thrumpton, a hamlet in the parish of Ordsall; the houses in South Retford, run along the Boundary of East Retford, and extend Southward until they join Thrumpton, so as to form almost one continued line of buildings. West Retford is divided from East Retford by the River Idle; the bridge over this is in direct continuation of the streets of both of these Towns, which present the appearance of one Town only. The houses of East and West Retford have a respectable appearance; there is no manufactory of any kind in the Town, which depends entirely for its support upon the retail trade carried on with the inhabitants of the surrounding agricultural districts.

The principal increase to the Town seems to be taking place in what is now called South Retford, a suburb on the Tuxford Road, and without the present Borough.

We recommend the annexation of the populations of these suburbs to the Borough. The line proposed will be nowhere more than one mile distant from the Town, and will include no great portion of agricultural district.

3. There is no Borough Rate in the nature of a County Rate; the Borough Rating. contributes to that for the County of Nottingham. This is taken out of the Poor Rate; it amounts—

In East Retford, to £.92. 16. 6. in the year, which is 3¾d. in the pound.
   West Retford, to £.40   -   „   „   -   7¾d.   „
   Clarborough, to £.125   -   „   „   -   6¾d.   „
   Ordsall, to £.74. 16. 9.   -   „   „   -   6¼d.   „

The Poor Rate Assessment, however, is unequal in these Townships:

   In East Retford, it is estimated at one-third the rack rent;
   In West Retford, at one-half for houses, and full value for land;
   In Clarborough, at two-thirds on land, and one-half for houses;
   In Ordsall, at one-fourth for houses, and nearly full value for land.

4. The Police consists of two Serjeants at Mace, sworn in as Constables.   The   Police.
latter are paid by the Corporation, for any additional duty caused by elections or
other extraordinary causes, from 40l. to 50l. a year.   A Rate will probably be
requisite for a more efficient Police.

5. The Streets of the Town of East Retford are repaired partly by the Corpora-   Paving and
tion, and partly by rate under the General Highway Acts, which is generally about   Lighting.
1 s. in the pound on the Poor Rate assessment.

The proposed new boundaries — the official report.

EAST
RETFORD.   REPORTS FROM COMMISSIONERS:

Rate Payers.   6. The following is a Statement of the Number of Persons rated for Houses and
                   other Buildings in the Borough, and parts proposed to be annexed to it:—

	Rate Payers, 1835.	Householders.	Rate Payers, 1835-4.	Householders.	Rate Payers, 1835-4-3.	Householders.
East Retford - •	509					
West Retford - -	81 *	81	80	80	80	80
Moorgate and Spittal} Hill - - -}	282 †	280	280	278	280	278
Thrumpton - -	48 ‡	41	38	31	35	28
Proposed Borough -	920					

   * Besides this number, there are 21 houses for which three persons only are rated as landlords,
and who are also included in the 81 as rate-payers for other houses; six of the 81 are females.
   † Of the above 282, eight are landlords, rated for about 80 houses occupied by tenants; 27 are
females.   There are, besides the above, 13 unoccupied houses.
   ‡ Nine of these are females.

Burgesses.   7. The number of Burgesses registered for the present Borough is 234.

                   We recommend that the Boundary of the new Borough should be as follows:—

PROPOSED   From the Northernmost Point (1) at which the River Idle meets the
BOUNDARY.   Boundary of the Hamlet of Moorgate, Eastward, along the said Boundary
                   to the Southernmost Point (2) at which the same crosses the Chesterfield
                   Canal; thence, Southward, along the said Canal to the Point (3) at which
                   the same meets the Boundary of the old Borough; thence in a straight Line
                   to a Point (4) in Cut-throat Lane, which is distant Three hundred and
                   twenty-four Yards (measured Eastward along such Lane), from the Point at
                   which the same leaves the Tuxford Road; thence in a straight Line to the
                   Point (5) at which the Tuxford Road meets Brick-kiln Lane; thence, South-
                   ward, along the Tuxford Road to the Point (6) at which the same meets the
                   Road leading from the Tuxford Road to Ordsall; thence, Westward, along
                   the said Road to Ordsall to the Point (7) at which the same crosses the River
                   Idle; thence, Northward, along the River Idle to the Aqueduct (8) by which
                   the Chesterfield Canal crosses the River Idle; thence, Westward, along the
                   said Canal to a Point (9) which is distant Six hundred Yards (measured
                   Westward along such Canal) from the Point at which the same crosses the
                   Worksop Road; thence in a straight Line to the Point first described.

                                                       Harry D. Jones.
                                                       D. Maude.
                        The Commissioners' reports and recommendations.

Boundaries of the Borough.

Ordsall village, with gaslamps and drainage works among the changes brought by the Borough.

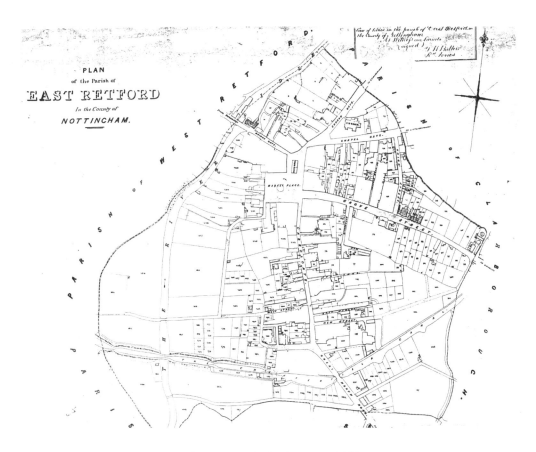

The East Retford tithe map of 1850.

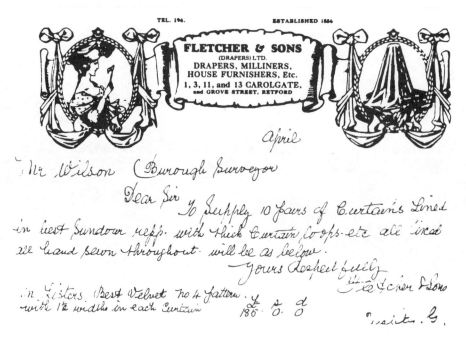

Curtains for the new Town Hall?

The ballroom in the new Town Hall.

The crystal chandeliers above the grand staircase came from Rufford Abbey.

The Council Chamber — two of its chandeliers came from the old Town Hall.

A fine view of the Town Hall.

GAS COMMITTEE :

His Worship the Mayor (Councillor W. R. HOWELL).

   Alderman J. THORNTON, *Chairman.*

      ,,   A. P. WILLIAMSON, *Vice-Chairman.*

      ,,   W. N. BRACKETT.

      ,,   S. H. CLAY.

      ,,   JOHN PEATFIELD.

   Councillor R. C. CLARK.

      ,,   B. HAIGH.

      ,,   G. T. PHILLIPSON.

      ,,   J. R. PLANT.

J. R. BRADSHAW, B.Sc. (Eng.),
Engineer and Manager.

The Gas Committee, 1920.

*An advertisement for W.J. Jenkins & Co, Retford's
Gas Works engineers.*

" Whereas the several persons, parties to these presents, have agreed to form a Company to be called the Retford Gas and Coke Company for the purpose of manufacturing and supplying gas in order to light the streets, ways, lanes, and other public passages and places of the town of East Retford aforesaid, and of Clarboro', West Retford, and Ordsall in the County of Nottingham and any adjoining township or townships either by contract or agreement with the Inspectors appointed or to be appointed by virtue of an Act of Parliament passed in the third and fourth year of the reign of his present Majesty, King William the Fourth . . . . and for lighting the shops, private houses, and public and private buildings in the said townships."

The deed of settlement for the Retford Gas & Coke Co.

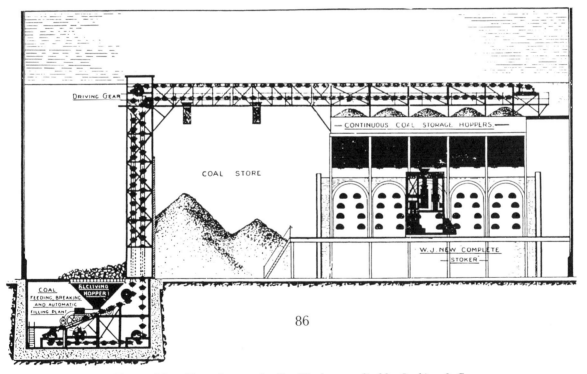

86

The coal-handling plant at the Gas Works, supplied by Jenkins & Co.

Retford Gas Works in 1920.

Health and Efficiency

AS the 19th century drew to its close life in Retford was that of a pretty country town for some, in which residents lived the good life; for others, squalor and disease lurked behind the elegant facades. As always, much depended upon personal circumstances; those who lived in the fine Georgian houses that lined Grove Street and the Square were obviously considerably more comfortable than the families crammed into the tiny rooms of slum terraces that existed in all parts of the town. Canal Row, Beardsalls Row and the courtyards of the Galway Arms and other inns, where car parking spaces now take the place of tiny cottages, were where people lived in close proximity to pigsties, stables and manure heaps.

When it came to water supplies and sanitation, everyone faced the same problems. Until the Borough Council set up its water works in 1880, there was no piped water supply and even then many years were to pass before every household was connected to the mains. Sanitation was virtually non-existent, the better-off would pay a contractor to regularly empty their privies, and this was carried out after dark or early in the morning; hence the term 'night soil'. The contractors, or scavengers as they were known, would go round the town with their horse-drawn carts collecting their noisome loads, to be taken to the canal wharf, spilling much of it on the way. At the wharf it would be heaped up to await loading on to boats to be taken away for spreading on the land as manure. Many were the complaints about the appalling smell from the wharf, and not least from the boatmen who had to load and unload the stuff.

For those who could not afford the contractors' fees the answer was to bury it in the garden or, as many did, throw it into the streets along with the sink water. It is not surprising that the town was unhealthy and that outbreaks of cholera and similar illnesses often occurred. A Public Health Act had been passed as early as 1858 but not much happened in Retford until a Board of Health was set up in 1866. The first thing they did was to appoint a Surveyor, and Inspector of Nuisances at an annual salary of £25 with instructions to 'inspect all the places in the town with a view to removing all nuisances'. He would immediately have become the most unpopular person in the Borough as he tried to enforce the bye-laws.

The night soil contractors were soon in trouble and faced legal proceedings for scattering filth on the streets, and eventually the Borough Council took over. At first they employed contractors but later employed their own men. Also threatened with legal enforcement notices were the various owners of properties, particularly those at Canal Row, regarding the provision of adequate water supplies and of privies. But the most unpopular and hardest bye-law to enforce was that made on 13 July 1868 which required every household equipped with a water pump to work it for a period of not less than half an hour every morning, between the hours of 8 and 9 o'clock, for the purposes of flushing the drains and ditches. As only the larger houses possessed pumps that meant another job for the servants.

Eventually the Board of Health became the Sanitary and Highways Committee of the East Retford Borough Council, with far-reaching powers of enforcement. There were 23 miles of public roads, including five miles of the Great North Road, within the Borough and all were described in 1881 as being in a bad condition, most being little more than stony tracks. Great excitement was caused when a 10 ton steam road roller arrived from Aveling and Porter of Rochester on a month's trial, the terms 35s (£1.75p) per day plus the cost of coal and water, which was estimated at 5s (25p) per day. Aveling and Porter provided the driver and, on days when the roller was not working, the hirer was to pay 5s (25p) to cover his wages. The spectacle of a new-fangled steamroller at work in place of the old horse-drawn roller drew crowds of onlookers and brought greatly improved roads.

After a two month trial, the Council purchased the steamroller and employed its own driver. Soon it was receiving requests from other towns to hire it, such as Doncaster and Worksop, as well as the Clumber Estate. It charged a daily rate many times greater than that of the manufacturers but, as more steamrollers were sold, so the charges had to be reduced, and in 1897 the Rural District Council was only asked to pay 18s (90p) per day, 'they finding coal, oil for the engine and lodgings for the driver and flag lad'. The roller, which was kept in a shed on the canal wharf, was finally sold for £75 in 1904, when it was replaced by a new one.

In 1884 the conditions at Canal Row were still giving cause for concern to the Borough Surveyor who reported 'I think it very desirable that something is done quickly in this unwholesome district. It is highly necessary that the inhabitants should have every inducement to keep themselves and their premises cleaned'. For those who had the misfortune to live in Bethel Chapel Yard it must have been impossible to maintain decent standards. A report of 1884 given by the Surveyor said 'I have visited the two cottages in the Bethel Chapel yard, both are very dilapidated. The first contains a ground floor living room 10ft x 11ft x 7ft high, a small back room used as a pantry, a loft in the roof which has scant provision for light and ventilation and just sufficient height to stand up in the highest part is used as a sleeping room. This house is occupied by James Allen, his wife and 5 children.

'The second house has a living room about 10ft x 11ft and a pantry but no bedroom, it is occupied by John Bell, his wife and 3 children.' Both houses were certified as being unfit for human habitation.

1884 could be described as the year of the great stench. The cause of the problem was a ditch that acted as the main drain for the gas works and all the houses on Grove Street, Union Street, Spital Hill and a large part of Moorgate. On 12 August the Inspector of Nuisances was visited by Mr Ostick in his capacity as Secretary of the Trustees of the United Free Methodist chapel, who said that during the Sunday evening service the stench was simply unbearable and that several people in the congregation were ill from the effects.

The inspector came up with an ingenious scheme to flush the ditch regularly with water from the canal, but he was blocked by the canal manager, who would not agree to the loss of water. This was countered by the Council offering to dredge and deepen the canal water feeder stream from the river Idle at its own expense, so as to compensate for any water used in flushing the ditch, but still the Canal Company would have none of it, so presumably the stink continued in dry, hot weather. When it came to road-sweeping however, the inspector was more successful, as he was able to persuade the Council to purchase a 'Patent One Horse Street Sweeper' at a cost of £34, which he advised was more efficient than hand sweeping.

By 1888 the use of steam power was causing a smoke problem and many complaints were received by the Council. Their answer was to bring in a new bye-law about chimney heights, and Charles Clark of Grove Street, who used a 3hp engine at his laundry and dye works, was ordered to raise his chimney from 30ft to 60ft. Charles Bailey's Britannia Works, with an 18hp engine, was told to have an 80ft chimney, as was Joseph Thornton of south Retford. Smith and Nephew were given permission to build a new boiler-house at their Carolgate brewery, provided they gave it a sufficiently high chimney to carry the smoke away. All of this seems to have had little effect, for the complaints, like the smoke, still poured forth in 1895.

Pigs were another major problem for the Sanitary Committee in the 1890s, because people would persist in keeping them in their town centre yards. One of the worst offenders was a Mr Unsworth, who was a mineral water manufacturer and ale and porter bottler, with works in a yard adjoining the Turks Head in Grove Street. In the same yard he insisted upon keeping many pigs and, if mineral waters, beer bottling and pig manure seem an unfortunate combination, it should also be known that William Unsworth was in addition an undertaker and hired out horse-drawn carriages. Many of the crude glass bottles that were used by Unsworths still exist, having been dug up in gardens or dredged out of the canal or the Idle.

Compared to today, Retford's postal services were far superior in the year 1900 but, with no telephones, letters were the only means of communicating with the outside world. The main post office was in Bridgegate and its opening hours were from 7am to 9pm Monday to Saturday and 8 to 10 on Sunday mornings. Anything up to four deliveries a day were made in the town and there were sub-offices at London Road and Queen Street.

Before radio or television were invented everyone relied upon the newspapers to keep them informed but local news was then usually considered more important than the fact that yet another country had been added to the British Empire, or such foreign matters. Retford in 1900 was supporting three local newspapers the *Retford, Worksop, Isle of Axholme and Gainsborough News* was published from Carolgate every Friday. The *Retford and Gainsborough Times* had its home in the Market Place, while the *Retford and Worksop Herald* was based in Exchange Buildings; they also published every Friday. Every morning the national newspapers would arrive by train from London and Manchester.

Politics had been a pre-occupation of Retford people for many years, but now the interest was less parochial and did not involve bribery at election times. The Liberals established a Retford club in 1883 and soon after moved to premises in Grove Street, but they were preceded by the Conservatives, who formed a local club in 1878 and by 1899 claimed to have 600 members. Party politics did not officially affect local government for many more years, for most candidates standing for election as councillors on the Borough or Rural District councils did so as independents.

Because of its role as the trading capital of a large part of Nottinghamshire, banking had always been important to Retford. It is believed that the town's first bank was that licensed in 1813 and known locally as Foljambe's, because its resident partner was Mr Francis Thornagh Foljambe; other partners were Sir William Cooke and Messrs Parker and Walker. In 1850 Mr H.B.W. Milner, father of Major Milner of West Retford House, and Mr Granville Harcourt Vernon of Grove Hall became partners. Following the retirement of two of the partners in 1868 the business was transferred to Becketts Bank. The bank was at 17 The Square, next door to the present Town Hall, and its resident partner used to live in the rooms above the public offices; to the rear was an extensive walled garden.

Next door was another bank, known as the Nottingham and Nottinghamshire Banking Co, and in the early 1900s both were merged with another company which by 1923 was trading as the Westminster Bank at 21 The Square. In 1926 East Retford Borough Council was desperate for offices and purchased the old bank premises for £7,250 and it was soon after that the present ornate frontage was added, together with the crest of the Borough and the words 'Old Bank'. The building's long association with money matters continues to this day, as it is used for the receipt of payments to the District Council.

What is now the National Westminster Bank at 21 The Square started life as a private house complete with coach houses, stables, granaries and its own brewhouse. Its garden ran down to the river Idle and had hothouses with grapevines, and on its south-facing walls were fig trees and espalier pear trees. In 1827 it was purchased for £2,000 by Gervase King Holmes, who was to become the first Mayor of the Borough; he sold it in 1841 to the part-time Town Clerk of East Retford, William Newton, who demolished the old house and built a new one. He sold that to the Nottingham and Notts Bank in 1876 for £4,000 and under NatWest management the premises have been extensively altered and enlarged.

Although still primarily a country market town, Retford at the beginning of the 20th century already had several important factories, each employing many people and all nationally-known companies. The Northern Rubber Company had been established in 1871 by Alfred Pegler and, by the mid-1900s, was employing several hundred people. In 1896 W.J. Jenkins took over the works of Hopkinsons, which manufactured machinery used in various processes; British Ropes came later to the Retford area, not opening their wire mill until 1916. One of Retford's most famous companies was that of Clark's the dyers and dry cleaners which, from small beginnings in a Grove Street yard, had expanded to a large organisation with some 50 branch shops and a factory at Hallcroft employing about 400 staff.

In spite of such large-scale developments, the old way of life continued much as it had for centuries, with Retford acting as the centre of its immediate area. Produce and cattle sales were still held in the Square, the town's traders acted as wholesalers to the village shops and people came here to make their special purchases, such as furniture, jewellery, clocks and watches, or the latest household gadgets like hand-operated washing machines, mangles and carpet sweepers.

Although the railways had killed the stage-coach traffic, carriers' carts were still lumbering into town as late as 1920. They provided a valuable service to the villagers, by collecting and delivering parcels and messages. Many were the village women who would give the carrier a note bearing vital measurements, to be delivered to such as J.R. Plant at his drapers' shop in the Market Place. The following week the carrier would return with a discreetly wrapped parcel containing a specially made whalebone corset, if that was what had been ordered.

Each carrier had his appointed place of arrival and departure: those for Clayworth and Gringley on the Hill used the Vine Inn; for Wiseton, Sturton le Steeple and Askham, the Crown Hotel. Others made use of the stables and yards at inns such as the Granby, Sun and the Black Boy.

Henry Spencer and Sons, the auctioneers who were to become world-famous in the antiques market, were still advertising themselves as specialists in agricultural work and held livestock sales every Monday in Retford Cattle Market and on Saturdays in the Market Place. Edgar Welchman advertised his services as a photographic artist and picture framer, and many years were to pass before the family would turn its attention to radios, electrical goods and then television.

Smith Foster and Company of the Square were leading grocers, wine and spirit merchants and in Cannon Square the Household Supply Stores offered for sale oil lamps of all kinds and low cost lamp glasses, gas light globes, tinware, wallpaper and 'everything for the household'. Willows were already established as high-class gentlemen's outfitters and Norths the Chemists had been established for 140 years. Occupying much of Grove Street was Howard's Commercial and Temperance Hotel and restaurant where hot dinners and teas were served daily. G. Howard and Son were also grocers, caterers, bakers and confectioners, making daily deliveries to all parts of the town. They were often described as the Fortnum and Mason of Retford.

Welchman's are not the only business to have changed direction over the years; for example, Swannack's of Bridgegate used to be builders and carpenters and Oates in the Square were ironmongers, then seed merchants and pet food suppliers before finally selling out.

Coal had been discovered in rich seams near Retford and a model village was built at Harworth to house miners. A writer in 1920 claimed that coal had also been found at Hayton, Cottam and Leverton and was confident that the town would soon become an important and prosperous mining centre. Fortunately his prediction was wrong and Retford remained a country market town.

Harworth Colliery in 1914.

A class at King Edward VI Grammar School taken in 1917.

Edwardian Empire Day in The Square.

The market in 1908.

The Royal visit to Retford, outside the Town Hall, on 26 June 1914.

The entrance gates to King's Park, 1937.

A horse-drawn fire engine of the type used at Retford.

The Laneham Express carrier heads for Retford market.

BYELAWS

RELATING   TO

KINGS'   PARK,   RETFORD

made under Section 164 of the Public

Health Act, 1875

BYELAWS

made under section 164 of the Public Health Act,
1875, by the Mayor, Aldermen and Burgesses of
the Borough of East Retford acting by the Council
with respect to the pleasure ground known as
Kings' Park, Retford.

Bye-laws for King's Park.

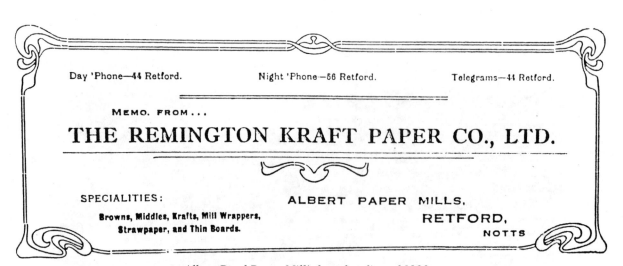

Day 'Phone—44 Retford.   Night 'Phone—56 Retford.   Telegrams—44 Retford.

MEMO. FROM...

THE REMINGTON KRAFT PAPER CO., LTD.

SPECIALITIES: ALBERT PAPER MILLS,

Browns, Middles, Krafts, Mill Wrappers,   RETFORD,
Strawpaper, and Thin Boards.   NOTTS

Albert Road Paper Mill's letterheading of 1930.

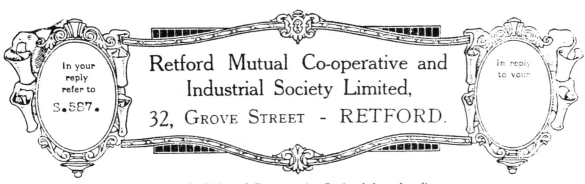

In your reply refer to S.587.

Retford Mutual Co-operative and Industrial Society Limited, 32, GROVE STREET - RETFORD.

In reply to your

The Retford Mutual Co-operative Society's letterheading.

Designs and Estimates Submitted.
Monuments Cleaned & Repaired.

Established over a Century.

Showyard: Shell Cottage.
London–Road, Retford.

SHARPE & HOGGARD

DESIGNERS & WORKERS IN MARBLE, GRANITE, STONE AND SLATE.

Monumental and General Masons,
THE OLD WORKS,
NEW STREET
RETFORD.

LETTER CUTTING OUR SPECIALITY.

Sharpe & Hoggard's letterheading.

ALL COMMUNICATIONS TO BE ADDRESSED TO THE COMPANY AND NOT TO INDIVIDUALS.

TELEGRAPHIC ADDRESS:
"JENKINS, RETFORD.

LONDON OFFICE:
17, VICTORIA STREET, S.W.1
TEL No. VICTORIA 5061

CODES USED:
WESTERN UNION A B C 5TH EDITION.

NATIONAL TELEPHONE:
NOS. 131 & 132 RETFORD.
PRIVATE BRANCH EXCHANGE.

W. J. JENKINS & Co., LTD.,

GAS AND CONSTRUCTIONAL ENGINEERS,
IRON AND BRASS FOUNDERS.

SOLE MAKERS OF
DE BROUWER PATENT
STOKING MACHINERY AND
COKE CONVEYORS.

MAKERS OF ALL CLASSES OF
COAL & COKE HANDLING PLANTS.

COKE RAMS & LEVELLERS.

COMPLETE GAS PLANTS.

PLEASE REPLY TO

BEEHIVE WORKS,

RETFORD, 18th., October 1922.

NOTTS.

YOUR REF.

(PLEASE QUOTE)
OUR REF   IF/TH.

Jenkin's letter to the Town Clerk about the Gas Works.

Established 1779.

Market Square,
RETFORD, Dec 31st 1930

'Phone 80

Mr. F. Colton.   Sherwood.   Holly Rd.

In account with F. J. NORTH, M.P.S.
CHEMIST.

Drugs, Medicines, and Chemicals of the Highest Quality.

Horse and Cattle Medicines.   Photographic Materials.

A bill from North's the chemist.

Rural District Council of East Retford

Any reply to this communication
should be addressed to—
THE CLERK TO THE EAST RETFORD
RURAL DISTRICT COUNCIL
at the address shewn.

S/SH

1, LEVERTON ROAD,

RETFORD, NOTTS.

16th November, 1932.

Dear Sir,

<u>Treasurer of the Council</u>

As requested by you, I send you the
following copy of the resolution of my Council passed
at their meeting on the 27th August, 1932 :-

"<u>TREASURER</u>"

"A letter dated 4th August from Mr.
"V. H. Brameld was submitted resigning the office of
"Treasurer of the Council, and it was <u>resolved</u> that
"the same be accepted with an expression of this
"Council's appreciation of the services rendered by
"Mr. Brameld in that capacity.

"It was further <u>resolved</u> to appoint
"the Westminster Bank Limited as Treasurer of the
"Council with effect from 1st September, 1932."

Yours faithfully

Clerk to the Council.

The Manager,
Westminster Bank Limited,
RETFORD.

The Rural District of East Retford appoints a Treasurer.

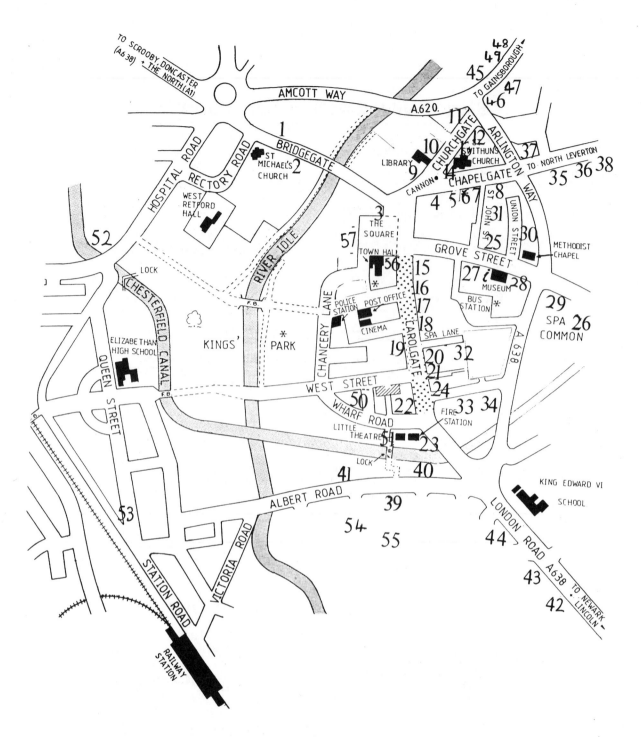

Retford's inns, taverns and hotels: key —
Bridgegate 1 Galway Arms, 2 Newcastle arms, 3 White Hart Hotel; *Chapelgate* 4 Crown Hotel, 5 Olde Sun,
6 Blacks Head, 7 Sportsman, 8 Victoria; *Churchgate* 9 Vine, 10 Ram, 11 Portland Arms, 12 Sherwood Rangers,
13 Ordsall Brewery Vaults, 14 Comet; *Carolgate* 15 Marquis of Granby, 16 Butchers Arms, 17 Brewers Arms,
18 Imperial Crown, 19 Red Lion, 20 Talbot, 21 White Swan, 22 Anchor, 23 Bridge Inn, 24 Pheasant Hotel;
Grove Street 25 Turks Head, 26 Packet Inn, 27 Redford Arms, 28 Royal Oak, 29 Cricketers; *Union Street*
30 Robin Hood; *St John Street* 31 Fox Inn; *Spa Lane* 32 Durham Ox; *New Street* 33 Prince of Wales, 34 Globe;
Spital Hill 35 Masons Arms, 36 Plough, 37 Sun, 38 Canal Tavern; *Albert Road* 39 Albert, 40 Clinton Arms,
41 Moulders Arms; *London Road* 42 Railway Inn, 43 Oddfellows, 44 Joiners Arms; *Moorgate* 45 Red Lion,
46 George, 47 Black Boy, 48 Brick and Tile, 49 Queens Head; *Wharfe Road* 50 Ship Inn, 51 Navigation;
Hospital Road 52 Boat Inn; *Queens Road* 53 Queens Hotel; *Thrumpton* 54 New Inn, 55 Riflemans Arms;
The Square 56 Half Moon, 57 Angel.

Beer and Skittles

IF there is any one subject that is likely to cause discussion, or even argument, in any ancient town it is the story of its inns. No matter how diligently a researcher may study the old directories and records in an attempt to trace the details of every public house that still exists, or may at one time have existed, it is virtually impossible to compile a complete list. Many are those who think they have succeeded only to be told that they have missed out a Red Lion or some such pub that somebody's grandfather used to talk about. And many inns changed their names, thus confounding confusion.

Retford has had so many inns it would be possible to fill a book with their stories, especially when it is realised that in the 1800s there were at least 56 premises selling alcoholic drinks. Perhaps the easiest way is to look at the inns by roads as this also helps to see why they came about.

The first main road through Retford was along Bridgegate, through what we know as Cannon Square and along Chapelgate. Thirsty travellers could call at the Mermaid which stood in Bridgegate. This inn became notorious for its disease-ridden yard, crowded with broken-down outbuildings in which lived people, horses, pigs and chickens without proper drainage. All that was cleared away when Bridgegate was rebuilt by the Trinity Hospital trustees and its place taken by the neat and tidy Galway Arms, named after the Lords Galway of Serlby Hall near Scrooby.

Also in Bridgegate the Newcastle Arms has always been important to West Retford; it never became a leading coaching inn but was popular with carriers and, during Retford's lively elections in the early 1800s, was where the supporters of the Duke's candidates would gather for their free drinks. Apart from the White Hart, the next inn was the Crown in Cannon Square, for many years Retford's leading hotel and believed to have been a licensed house since 1646. To cater for increasing business its owners in 1754 demolished the original thatched roofed building and erected a fine Georgian hotel with ample stables, an assembly room and comfortable rooms for overnight accommodation. The Crown was on occasions used as a court by magistrates and for meetings of the Council while the new Town Hall was built.

At Retford's old-style elections the Crown would become the headquarters of one of the candidates, although that must have been a mixed blessing, for on more than one occasion unruly mobs smashed windows and burnt furniture. For a few years the Crown was a leading coaching inn but lost that trade to the White Hart when the Great North Road was diverted through Retford in 1766. In more recent years, when Retford was crowded with off-duty servicemen during the last war, the Crown was one of their favourite meeting places. Packed into its upstairs concert room they would take part in lively 'Vera Lynn' style sing-songs, which could be heard all over that part of the town on Saturday evenings.

After the war had ended and the servicemen had departed the Crown slowly but surely declined in importance and eventually was closed to re-emerge as the offices of a building society. However in recent years the former Crown Hotel has risen again and is once more serving food and drink, but under a new name, that of the Litten Tree.

Perhaps, if anyone is in the building and they listen carefully, they may hear some sounds of the past, maybe the voice of an 18th century magistrate sentencing a thief to be 'whipped round the town till his back be bloody', or snatches of an old election speech mixed in with voices singing 'we'll meet again'.

Across the road from the Crown stands the Vine, another inn popular with carriers, still open and where customers still pass under its archway to reach the bars. One of its upstairs windows is still bricked up due to the window tax repealed in 1851. At the rear of its long courtyard in the 1880s the innkeeper ran a hay and straw business.

Chapelgate's Olde Sun is one of Retford's oldest buildings; formerly a private house, it was turned into an inn during the 1750s and, as the years went by, gained the prefix of 'Ye Olde'. Immediately next door stood the Black Head and further along the road were the Sportsman, the Victoria and a beerhouse. In addition to the Vine, Churchgate had its Ram, Portland Arms and the Sherwood Rangers as well as the Ordsall Brewery Vaults at number 4 and the Comet.

People travelling along Carolgate had no need to go thirsty as it also had plenty of inns including the Marquis of Granby, Butchers Arms, Brewers Arms, Imperial Crown, Red Lion, Talbot, White Swan, Anchor and the Bridge Inn, not forgetting the Pheasant Hotel with its Retford and Worksop Brewery Company offices. Grove Street may now only have its Turks Head and Packet Inn but in the 1800s there was a choice between them and the Redford Arms, the Royal Oak and the Cricketers. The Packet Inn, built beside the canal to cater for passengers off the packet boats, was reconstructed in 1913, perhaps by its then owner who was by trade a builder. The directories are rather vague about the actual whereabouts of an inn called the Robin Hood; some say it was in the yard of the Turks Head while others put it firmly in Union Street perhaps the owners acquired new premises and took the name with them. The Fox Inn does not appear to be listed so perhaps it was only a beerhouse, as their names were rarely shown.

Along Spa Lane was the Durham Ox and New Street had its Prince of Wales and the Globe, the latter at the entrance to White's canal basin and wharf. In 1844 Spital Hill had a Freemasons Arms, a Plough and a Sun, by 1864 joined by a Canal Tavern; later the Freemasons shortened its name to the present Masons Arms. An 1864 directory shows the Clinton Arms on Alma Road and London Road as having a Manchester and Lincolnshire Railway Inn and an Oddfellows. Whitehouses then had two inns, namely the White House and the Nags Head. Moorgate, which before the inner ring road severed the two was a continuation of Churchgate, had a Red Lion, a George and a Blacks Head in addition to the remaining Brick and Tile, Queen's Head and Black Boy, or perhaps the latter is really the old Blacks Head. New developments brought the opportunities for new inns; the canal led to the opening of the Navigation beside Town Lock and the Ship Inn on Wharf Road. At West Retford near Woodcock's bridge was the Boat Inn, which for many years was presided over by Bilby Dixon, who served ale between running a wharf and being a coal merchant. The growth of Thrumpton brought the Albert Inn, the New Inn and the Rifleman's Arms.

In Victorian times every railway station had need of a hotel and, when the Great Northern Railway Company opened the present Retford station, an enterprising person erected the Queen's Hotel nearby, complete with stabling, comfortable accommodation and services for commercial travellers and families. Another newcomer in Victorian times was the Albert in Albert Road, both names relating of course to the Prince; a Moulders Arms is also listed for this road.

There are still inns in the heart of the town such as the Half Moon, which has been rebuilt and altered many times over the years. In 1844 there used to be a White Lion in the Market Place until its licence was transferred to new premises when West Street was built. At the same period the Half Moon and the Angel and Exchange Hotel (later to drop the Exchange part of its name) were open for business in the Square. But to the thousands of people who travelled on the Great North Road from 1766, Retford was the White Hart Hotel.

The White Hart began as a small tavern on the corner of Bridgegate as early as 1731 but, when the Great North Road was taken through Retford in 1766, its owners were quick to take advantage of the extra trade. The small inn was extended and for nearly 100 years was busy by day and night serving travellers. By 1828 at least 19 scheduled stage coaches on the London to north of England run stopped here to change horses and to set down or collect passengers and mail. Some of the coaches had romantic names like *The Rockingham* and *The Highflyer*.

From the north they would pass down Bridgegate under the White Hart archway into its cobbled courtyard, where ostlers and stable boys would leap into action. One team of horses would be quickly unharnessed to be replaced with ones fresh from the stables. Passengers would hurry into the hotel where refreshments were ready and waiting. But for those who were continuing their journey on the same coach, time for eating and drinking was limited for within a few minutes it was time to depart.

With a warning blast on the horn the coach would sweep out of the yard and across the Square to make its way down Carolgate and to its next stop at Tuxford. A good look-out would be kept for highwaymen on the lonely stretch across Markham Moor, where the notorious Dick Turpin had been known to strike. It is reputed that he was a regular caller at the White Hart, where he would sit quietly in a corner watching and assessing the wealth of the travellers passing through. Of far higher repute was the Dennett family, of whom several generations ruled the White Hart from 1818 for over 100 years and set the highest standards of service.

The welcome began in the courtyard where travellers were received by a uniformed head porter who would doff his top hat and bow to the important. Anyone who did not look suitable to be received at the White Hart would be quickly ordered to leave, and no locals were ever allowed to walk through the courtyard unless they were there on business. Even after the stage-coach era had ended, the same high standards of service and respectability were maintained for many more years. It is often claimed that the town was run from the exclusive 'gentlemen only' bar of the White Hart, to which only the privileged few were admitted.

Persons such as the Town Clerk and leading Councillors and Aldermen of the Borough would meet there every lunchtime, each with his appointed seat, and no one who was not of the 'set' was allowed in. If someone did make the mistake of entering that bar instead of the more public one he would not be served and was quickly asked to leave. When it snowed one of the first paths to he cleared was that which led from the Town Clerk's office across the Square to the hotel entrance.

With so many inns Retford needed a good supply of ale and in 1864 this was met by two local brewers. Just off Carolgate, along what is still known as Brewery Lane, was Thomas Hodgkinson's brewery. Later sold to Smith and Nephew, it became part of the Worksop & Retford Brewery Company that in turn was taken over by Tennant Brothers of Sheffield before becoming part of the Whitbread group. But brewing at Carolgate had ceased many years prior to that. In competition with Thomas Hodgkinson in 1864 was Samuel Cliffe's Cobwell Brewery, bought by a John Hewitt and later known as the Ordsall Brewery. In turn it was taken into the Hewitt Brothers of Grimsby's empire and ultimately acquired by Bass Charrington. A club in the old brewery building along Cobwell Road is all that now survives of a once busy place, apart from the Northern Inn just along the road, which perhaps used to be known as the Brewery Tap.

Although drinking seems to have taken up a lot of time in old Retford, people still found time to take part in sport and other entertainment. The first organised cricket matches were held by the town's apprentices on Spa Common with the full blessing of the Corporation. When a lessee of the land tried to stop the matches being held there in 1830, he was taken severely to task by the Town Council and warned that his lease would not be renewed if he caused further problems.

Until the Council built the Albert Road Baths, those who liked to go swimming had the dubious pleasure of using the river Idle or local ponds; small boys on very hot days would go 'skinny dipping' in the canal until they were ordered out. By the early 1900s various sporting clubs and organisations had been formed, such as the Retford Bowling Green Club. The Retford Sports Club provided facilities for tennis, cricket, football and bowling, the Retford Town Football Club belonged to the Central Football Alliance and Retford Cricket Club played in the Bassetlaw League.

Golf enthusiasts who belonged to the Retford Golf Club opened a nine hole course on West Carr Hills in 1921 and freshwater fishermen took up their stations all along the Chesterfield Canal and the river Idle, with the Retford Angling Association having exclusive rights on the canal from West Retford to Ranby. Until pollution occurred during the 1914-18 war, there was excellent trout fishing to be had in the river Idle and a flourishing River Idle Fly Fishing Club.

Hunting, although then a sport for the wealthier, was actively followed by many who would eagerly turn up at meetings and from carefully chosen vantage points hope to see the pack in pursuit. Both the Grove and the Rufford Hunts met in the Retford area and, until recent years it was the tradition for a hunt to begin in the Square at Retford every Boxing Day.

A delightful account of an outing held by the Speedwell Cycling Club in 1893 survives. It tells us that, after leaving the Market Square, they rode out to the Chequers at Ranby, then on to the Normanton Inn and West Drayton before arriving for tea 'at the pretty Markham Clinton rectory as guests of our President the Revd Seymour Bentley'. After tea they returned to Retford 'along darkening tree lined lanes'. In 1902 the annual subscriptions to the club were 2s 6d (12p) for gentlemen and 1s (5p) for ladies.

Retford's first theatre was opened as early as 1789 and was along Carolgate. It was quite small and was never looked upon as important enough to be included on the tours of leading companies. All kinds of theatrical performances were held there, ranging from Shakespeare to Victorian drama and comedy. This theatre existed for some 50 years but was then closed and the building became a Methodist chapel. Although musical concerts were held in the Town Hall and the assembly room of the Crown Hotel, many years were to pass before Retford could again claim to have a live theatre.

The cinema age brought a great choice of entertainment. At the Regent Theatre on Carolgate bridge in 1929 Gary Cooper starred in a film called *Wings*, which the programme said was about 'soldiers of the air'. Also showing was Buster Keaton in *The General*. The other cinemas were Picture House Theatre in Carolgate, which had tea rooms and a billiard hall and later became known as the Roxy, and the Picture Drome in Exchange Street, but Retford's finest cinema was the Majestic. Built as a theatre with boxes, and fully equipped to handle live productions onstage it is the only commercial cinema to survive. Sunday opening of the Majestic in 1946 provoked a public outcry and led to angry meetings; eventually the Town Council held a public meeting to resolve the matter at which a vote was taken. The result was 248 in favour and 158 against.

The Cinema sadly closed its doors in 1983. The bingo hall managed to continue for two more years when, for the first time since 1927 the Theatre was left unused. In 1986 a local businessman, Richard Busten, opened its doors again and created a two-screen cinema. The rear stalls was a 100 seat studio cinema and the circle, a 300 or so seat cinema with the front stalls being used for bingo. Sadly, further closure followed and this time the future of the Majestic Theatre looked very bleak indeed as the cost of even basic maintenance was too high to make the theatre a viable business venture. In 1993, just when the building looked as if it was heading for demolition, a small group of Retford people set up the Majestic Theatre Trust. The aim of this group was to raise enough money to buy the theatre, save it from further deterioration and to see live performances on the grand stage once more. Sadly, the building had already fallen into a serious state of disrepair. A few fund raising shows were held but the theatre had to close until modern safety standards could be met. Fund raising continued, even though the theatre could not be used as a live venue. Much of the early restoration was provide by a small but dedicated team of volunteers. Generous donations of building materials and labour were often supplied by local businesses. The task facing the volunteers was at times daunting. The 4 foot sound proofed wall which separated the front stalls from the rear stalls had to be removed. Extensive repairs and remedial work was done to the circle to comply with 1997 fire regulations. Much of this work took place during The Yorkshire TV 'Action Time' programme between September 1997 and February 1998. This programme provided vital impetus to complete the restoration and re-opening of the Majestic.

The stained glass mermaid window in the upper bar area was added during the filming of the TV programme. The original plaster mermaids are still to be viewed in the main auditorium and have been restored to their former glory. A list of companies and organisations which took part and contributed to the project with their time, expertise and donations can be viewed in the upper bar foyer.

200 or so refurbished seats were acquired from A.J. Owen & Co, which had previously been installed in Saddlers Wells Theatre. The present seating capacity is 648 plus 4 wheelchair spaces.

Today the Majestic is going from strength to strength. It is completely run by unpaid volunteers to a high professional standard and is carving out a reputation with artists and public alike. Artists and production companies are keen and happy to perform in the theatre whilst the public are assured of a warm welcome and a varied program of entertainment whether it be local amateur productions or professional touring shows and artists.

Since its re-opening in 1997 The Majestic has played host to *Ken Dodd*, *Paul Daniels*, *Cannon and Ball*, *Max Boyce*, *Rick Wakeman*, *The Searchers*, *Slade*, *Joe Longthorne*, *Gerry & the Pacemakers*, and the *Syd Lawrence* and *Glen Miller Orchestras*,The theatre is also put to good use by local groups and schools such as The Retford Operatic Society, the Gilbert and Sullivan Society and numerous local dance schools.

The Retford Amateur Operatic Society began in 1920 and in the same year presented Gilbert and Sullivan's *The Mikado* at the Town Hall. Sixty-nine years on, several later members of the Society, having formed what they call the Generally G & S Society performed the same light opera, this time at the newly restored Majestic.

A Little Theatre group was set up in the 1940s and now has a purpose-built theatre which it leases from the District Council, where many productions are staged. The seating capacity of this intimate yet versatile theatre is up to 160. With an annual membership of over 1000, every performance plays to an enthusiastic audience.

Retford's Male Voice Choir has over the years become well known in many countries, their concerts often given in the fine Grove Street Methodist church.

Retford's foray into the modern age of night clubs has been less successful, and their presence has not been without problems. In 1967 one of the old canal warehouses was converted to become the Broken Wheel night club (not to be confused with the modern pub of the same name), followed by the Aquarius on River Lane and the Cats Cradle on Carolgate Bridge. Next came the Porterhouse in Carolgate and of the four, this is the sole survivor.

For such a relatively small town, Retford has always had a wide variety of societies, clubs and associations and most have been well supported.

The Newcastle Arms, Bridgegate.

The former Navigation Inn is the building to the right of Retford Town Lock.

The Galway Arms on Bridgegate.

FOR THIS NIGHT ONLY!!

THEATRE, RETFORD.

BENEFIT OF

MR. NANTZ.

On which occasion Mr. N. most respectfully solicits the honor of the Patronage of his Friends and the Public in general.

On SATURDAY Evening, February 22nd, 1834,

Will be presented, (POSITIVELY FOR THIS NIGHT ONLY,) Sheridan Knowles' celebrated Play of THE

HUNCHBACK

Master Walter, Mr. LEICESTER—Sir Thomas Clifford, Mr. NANTZ—Lord Tinsel, Mr. GORDON
Master Wilford, Mr. T. MANLY—Modus, Mr. ROBERTS—Master Heartwell, Mr. RILEY—Gaylove, Mr. GANNON
Fathom, Mr. BYFIELD—Thomas, Mr. CHALLENER—Holdwell, Mr. JONES—Stephen, Mr. GRINDELL—Servants

Julia, Miss CLARKSON—Helen, Mrs. ROBERTS

A FAVOURITE BALLAD, BY MISS BRITON.

A COMIC SONG, called "SARAH SYKES," BY Mr. BYFIELD.

The whole to conclude with (FOR THE FIRST TIME HERE,) a local, domestic, traditionary Melo Drama, entitled

ST. ANN'S WELL;

Or, "'Tis Ninety Years Since."

☞ WRITTEN BY MR. NANTZ, Author or "The Gibbet Law of Halifax," "The Brown Devil," "John Doe,"
"L'Cart," &c. &c,

"In the year 1795, a regiment of Dragoons lay at Nottingham, and at that time five of the men agreed to go a Deer stealing, for which purpose they traversed, in the night, over a great extent of country in vain. Chagrined at the disappointment, in passing over an eminence called Shepherd's Race, near St. Ann's Well, two of them agreed to go down to the Well and steal some of the geese belonging to the people who lived at St. Ann's Well. A young man, who was servant in the family, and had been out late in company, instead of going to bed, laid himself down upon a table in a room, or some other ready and convenient place, where he slept some time, but was awakened by the noise of the frightened geese, which were disturbed by the soldiers attempting to steal them. The young man, being a little elevated in liquor, had the temerity to go from the house, with an intent to protect his mistress's property, in which attempt he was shot through the head," &c.

A theatre bill of 1834.

Colonel Jackson, (of the —— regiment, quartered at Nottingham,) Mr. CLARKSON
Dennis O'Devilskin, (serjeant of the —— regiment,) Mr. T. MANLY
Hal Hutchinson, (private in the —— regiment,) Mr. LEICESTER
Cormorant Gobble, (private in the —— regiment, and a thorough-bred cockney, wit' a new Song, a parody on the "Soldier's Tear,") Mr. BYFIELD
Robin Goodfellow, (a native of Nottingham, waiter at "St. Ann's Well," and betrothed to Mary Booth,) Mr. NANTZ
Tom Booth, (a whitesmith and celebrated deer stealer,) Mr. ROBERTS
Benton, } Two Gamekeepers of the Snienton Coppices } Mr. GORDON
Samson, } Mr. GRINDELL
Coroner, Mr. CHALLINOR—Visitors to the Well, Soldiers, &c.

Dame Mallinson, (landlady of St. Ann's,) Miss CRAVEN—Mary Booth, (bar-maid of St. Ann's,) Miss CLARKSON

ACT I. Tap-room in the (——) public-house, Nottingham (!)

Devilskin and Gobble's ruminations on Hutchinson's affection for Mary Booth. Two ways of telling a tale, or which is the best? A soldier's view of a long journey and a glutton's anticipations after the same. Song, by Gobble, "A fig for the cares of this life." Rum reflections on a rum subject—*con-spirit*o. Prep—ations for deer stealing, and a *cutting* argument exemplified

EXTERIOR OF ST. ANN'S WELL, & PLEASURE GARDENS

Rencontre between Booth and the game-keeper of the park. More ways of killing a buck than one. A tale of the Leen Side Recrimination between Robin and Mary, a lover's hopes lie within the circumference of a *ring*. The Gypsey's story. Quar—rel between Robin and the soldiers. Arrival of Colonel Jackson—departure of the visitors from the Well—approach of night

PART OF THE COPPICES ON THE HILLS.

Exterior of "St. Ann's," and the Gardens by Moonlight.

Ill success of the deer stealers—more *cordial* receptions than one—preparations for robbing the Well—Gobble's affright—
Arrival of Booth—Alarm of the farm, and perpetration of a

HORRID MURDER!!!

ACT II. KITCHEN OF ST. ANN'S WELL.

Tableau of wretchedness—miserable situation of Booth, Mary, and Dame Mallinson, with the corpse—inhumanity of
Benton—a father's vengeance—arrival of the soldiers and

THE REAL MURDERER,

To arrest an innocent man—departure for Nottingham—peculiar situation of Cormorant Gobble, and terror of the Dame.

Road from St. Ann's Well to Nottingham.—LOCK-UP ROOM.

Gobble's hungry reflections—fall of man's greatness—and parody on "*THE SOLDIER'S TEAR.*" Meeting between
Hutchinson and Booth—arrest of Gobble—proud determination of Booth, and remorse and agony of the murderer.

BED CHAMBER IN ST. ANN'S WELL.

Mary's dream—clue to innocence—horror of Mary Booth at the

Appearance of Spectre of the Murdered Man!

AND MYSTERIOUS VANISHING!!!

EXTERIOR OF THE OLD TOWN HALL, NOTTINGHAM.

ROOM IN THE OLD TOWN HALL, NOTTINGHAM

Coroner's inquest on the body—examination of the witnesses—strength of circumstantial evidence—peculiar trial of touching
the corpse of the murdered man—condemnation of the innocent—awful denouement and

RETRIBUTIVE JUSTICE.

BOXES, 3s. PIT, 2s. GALLERY, 1s. Tickets and Places in the Boxes to be had of the Printer.
Also, of Mr. NANTZ, at Mr. C. C. Golland's, Bridge Gate.
Doors will open at Six o'Clock, and the Performance commence at half-past.

DEWHIRST, PRINTER, RETFORD.

LAST NIGHT OF MR. WILSON'S ENGAGEMENT.
Theatre Retford.
On Thursday Evening, November 5th, 1818.

Before the Play, Mr. WILSON will make

His Grand Ascension

ON THE TIGHT ROPE,
FROM THE STAGE TO THE GALLERY!
AND BACK, ENVELOPED IN A

Shower of Fire,

After the manner it was exhibited at VAUXHALL, in London, which attracted immense
Crowds every Evening during the whole of the last Season.

After which, (First time here,) the whimsical Petit Comedy, called

X, Y, Z.

Capt. Galliard, Mr. PINDER..... Grubbleton, Mr. CONNER,
Neddy Bray, Mr. SHEPPARD...Roscius Alldross, Mr. CLARKE...Doddle, Mr. BROWNE
Ralph Hemp-seed, Mr. PRITCHARD......1st. Gentleman, Mr. GILES
2nd. Gentleman Mr. MARTIN...3rd. Gentleman, Mr. GRIERSON
1st. Waiter, Mr. THOMAS...2nd. Waiter, Mr. JONES...... 3rd. Waiter, Mr. EARL
Maria, Miss SIDNEY...Mrs. Mouser, Mrs. SIDNEY
Betty, Miss HARGRAVE......Dora Mumwell, Miss PEIRCE

A Comic Song, by Mr. SHEPPARD.
Mr. WILSON will exhibit his astonishing Exertions on

The Tight Rope.

HE WILL COMMENCE WITH A
Scot's Dance in Character;
After which he will introduce several pleasing Equilibriums, and during his performance will throw an
EXTRAORDINARY

SOMERSAULT

Upon the descending part of the Rope over the Orchestra.
The novel and surp●ing Feat of
STANDING ON A CHAIR TURNED UPSIDE DOWN,
SUPPORTED BY
TWO QUART BOTTLES,
Which gave such unusual satisfaction during his Continental Tour, and never yet attempted by any
Person but himself. He will also dance his much admired FANDANGO, accompanying himself on the
CASTANETS, as composed expressly for him by Signor Baptiste, first Violin at the Theatre-Royal,
Madrid. To conclude with the favourite
TAMBOURINE RONDO.

After which, the humourous Farce of

Raising the Wind.

Diddler, Mr. PINDER——Fainwould, Mr CONNER——Sam, Mr. PRITCHARD
Plainway, Mr. WEBBER—Richards, Mr. BROWNE—Waiter, Mr. EARL
Peggy, Miss SIDNEY—Miss Lauretta Durable, Mrs. SIDNEY.

BOXES, 3s. PIT, 2s. GAL. 1s....... ...Half price BOXES, 1s. 6d. PIT, 1s.
Doors to open at half-past Five, and to begin at half-past Six o'Clock, (*Taylor, Printer.*)

A theatre bill of 1818.

The Blacks Head was decorated for Queen Victoria's 1897 Jubilee.

A circus bill of 1835, printed on silk.

The White Hart on Bridgegate in modern times.

The Majestic Theatre.

Ye Olde Sun, Retford's sole remaining timber-framed building.   *The Turk's Head.*

The Packet Inn today.

The Packet Inn was built in 1913 on the site of a much older one.

THE OLD THEATRE AT RETFORD

Near the centre of the west side of Carol-gate (Carhill Gate) there was a theatre erected in 1789, at the expense of Mr. Pero (then manager of this circuit), on ground purchased from Sir Thomas Woolaston White, Bart. After about half a century the building was converted into a Primitive Methodist Chapel. The area, which it occupied was very circumscribed, and, from a combination of circumstances, did not permit of any extension of the building.

The exterior has no pretensions to architectural beauty. The house was divided into two boxes, pit and gallery, the price of admission to these being three shillings, two shillings and one shilling respectively. The house held from £40 to £50. The Theatre was only opened during "the season" which varied in length.

Among the proprietors and managers were Messrs. Pero, Robertson, and Manby, names which are not unfamiliar to many Nottingham and other playgoers. From time to time many improvements were effected—the boxes were enlarged in 1800, and the threatre was decorated in 1827 by a Mr. Fraser.

The Retford theatre was ranked in the second class of country theatres. As Piercy has stated "this was one of the earliest provincial theatres that the celebrated Mr. Batty visited in his professional tour. Miss Frearson delighted the Retford audience before she appeared on the London stage, and Miss Foote, in 1827, gratified the admirers of the drama with a fine specimen of her abilities."

The bill of fare presented to the patrons of this theatre was greatly diversified, and included comedies, musical entertainments, tragedies, "favourite entertainment" farces, musical farces, "dramatic pieces," plays, "musical afterpieces," "grand spectacles," "favourite pieces," "dramatic dialogues," "celebrated and fashionable dramas," "comic operas," etc. The "scenic artist" at the end of last century was Mr. Robertson.

The Old Theatre, Retford — from the Retford Times.

The inner courtyard of the White Hart, where cars replace stagecoaches.

The Anchor.

St Swithun's church.

St Swithun can be seen in his niche in East Retford's Parish Church.

A Country Town

BY the 1930s the prospect of major industrialisation had passed for Retford. Certainly its existing factories were firmly established and more new businesses would arrive, but not on the scale to bring about any drastic changes in the character of the town. Changes were to follow, but they would come as the result of road alterations and a new form of local government.

Because of its mixed economy, Retford did not suffer too dramatically from the financial and trade depressions which preceded the outbreak of the Second World War. Many local people were unemployed and money was hard to come by, but compared to many towns it escaped the worst. War, with its demands for increased production in the factories and more home-grown food, obviously boosted Retford's economy. So too did the influx of thousands of servicemen, who were either travelling through on the A1 or stationed at camps nearby, such as the Army barracks at Ranby or Royal Air Force bases at Gamston, Bawtry and Scofton. Gamston alone accommodated nearly 2,000 Australian airmen in 1945.

Like all other towns Retford prepared for war as best it could. The old canal warehouse was converted to a civil defence headquarters, complete with gas decontamination showers. Air raid shelters were built at Amcott House and those who had not been called up joined the Home Guard or became air raid wardens, auxiliary firemen, or such. One of the first tasks to be undertaken by the Women's Voluntary Service was to organise the reception of hundreds of evacuee children, many of them coming from Great Yarmouth, and other vulnerable east coast towns, and from Leeds. Long hours were worked by men and women, both in the factories and on the land. The call by the Government to 'Dig for Victory' brought a big demand for more allotments.

In 1942 the call went out for more scrap metal, which was desperately needed to keep factories supplied. Retford's Street Salvage Stewards called upon the Town Council to remove the railings in the Square and the gun in Cannon Square, which had been given to the town after its capture from the Russians during the Crimean War in the 1850s. As a result the town lost most of its Victorian railings and the cannon was dismantled and taken away, but for some unknown reason it was never sent with the other scrap to be melted down. Instead it lay forgotten in somebody's yard until 1949, when it was restored to its present place of honour in Cannon Square.

Fortunately the town was not seen by the Germans as a major target and therefore escaped the misery and damage of air raids. However, the sound of aircraft was rarely absent, but it was the throb of Lancasters and other bombers as they passed over on their way to and from the Rhur, Berlin, Hamburg and other targets.

After the war came the drive to build houses, needed to ease the chronic shortage, and estates such as those at Hallcroft, Spital Hill and Ordsall began to take shape. Everywhere the shortage of goods caused problems for shops but, when the rest of the country's shopping high streets began to recover, Retford was slow to follow. It only ever succeeded in attracting branches of two major store groups, those of Woolworths and Boots. The others, such as Marks and Spencer, C&A and British Home Stores stayed away.

Until the town was by-passed by the A1 it was thought by many that it was the heavy traffic squeezing through narrow Bridgegate and Carolgate which was driving people away from Retford shops. Get rid of the traffic and all will be well, or so it was thought but, by the time that finally happened, it was too late, for other towns had already developed their new shopping centres, offering prices and a range of goods which Retford's older-style shops found hard to match.

Retford, unlike Newark, Grantham and Stamford, failed to become revitalised after the A1 had been removed. Instead it entered a period of decline. A visitor writing about the town in the 1970s claimed that it was a place where 'every day seemed as quiet as Sunday or the afternoon of early closing day.

No one seems to ever be in a hurry and urgency is unknown'. Even its once busy Co-operative Society departmental store had vast areas completely devoid of customers or staff.

Some roads became even quieter when a pedestrianisation scheme took through traffic away from Carolgate, Cannon Square, Churchgate and Chapelgate and the new inner ring road kept all but the most determined driver out of the town centre. Eventually a supermarket firm called Hillards decided to open a branch at the far end of Carolgate and erected a modern, flat-roofed building that will always be out of keeping with the town's traditional pantiled roofs and red brick gables. This had the effect of hastening the closure of the old-style grocery shops and the movement of shopping away from Bridgegate and the Square. Soon to follow was Boots, who closed their Market Place branch and moved into new premises built on the site of the old Roxy Cinema.

Retford Co-operative Society decided to merge with the Greater Nottingham Society, who demolished the old Carolgate store and built on the same site a large and successful supermarket, but its architecture was still strictly functional. While the new supermarkets were welcomed by most shoppers the loss of older shops continued and butchers, clothing, shoe shops and many others fell victim to the new retail patterns.

In 1974 the measures brought in by central government to re-organise local councils took effect and dealt to Retford what was seen by many as a hard blow. The theory was that, throughout the country, there were far too many small borough, urban and rural district councils, each with their own councillors, offices and staff. If many of them could be merged into larger units then great economies and streamlining of effort would inevitably result.

The Borough of East Retford was required to discuss a merger with its close neighbour, the East Retford Rural District Council, and with Worksop Borough and Worksop Rural District Councils. Of the four, Retford Borough was the oldest established council but in size of area and population it was the smallest. In the Council Chamber of Retford Town Hall the mood was one of gloomy resignation as it was realised that the town's centuries' old tradition of local rule was soon to be broken.

As is so often the case with modern minute books, those dealing with the meetings of the Borough Council held in the early 1970s are tantalizingly brief. If any stirring speeches opposing the merger were made they apparently went unrecorded, and anyway the public at that period was particularly bored with local government matters. The business of co-operating with the then shadow Bassetlaw District Council went quietly on and eventually the shadow became a reality. In 1974 the last meeting of East Retford Borough Council was held, 148 years after it had been formed and 728 years after its predecessor, the Corporation of East Retford, had by Royal assent begun to rule the town.

At first not much seemed to change, the same council offices remained open and were staffed by familiar people, but behind the scenes great difficulties were being encountered as the new authority tried to pull together the work of the four former councils, each with offices and depots scattered all over the area, into a single operation. There was one essential requirement; that of a new administration building, but the problem was where to build it. Quite naturally the councillors from the former Worksop authorities saw their town as the best location, yet in a report on the matter the Boundaries Commission advised that, because of its geographical position, Retford should house the administrative base of Bassetlaw District Council.

Various sites were proposed, such as West Retford Hall and park, Amcott House and its garden, Spa Common, Bridgegate, Eaton Hall and Ranby camp. Any of them would have involved new construction and some demolition, and they were all opposed for a variety of reasons by Retford people. It is easy now to be critical of that opposition and to claim that, by not supporting the proposals, Retford surrendered its chance to become the leading town of Bassetlaw. Obviously, to have had a large organisation such as the new District Council in the town, would have brought economic benefits and many job opportunities but, unless those who now criticise were involved at the time, how can they say what was right or wrong?

Unfortunately, the decision to build at Worksop was followed by plans to close practically all the council offices at Retford as soon as possible. When that happened the full effects of the merger became felt as Retford people, who for so many years had been used to a local council, found themselves having to travel to Worksop if they had a problem. Resentment at what was seen by many as a Worksop take-over gathered momentum and still has its exponents, although District Council offices covering most services have since been opened in Retford.

Although in the early 1980s it seemed that Retford was destined to drift into small town obscurity, a perceptible change had begun before the decade was over. People everywhere were rediscovering the charm and attractions of ancient market towns, some to visit as tourists, while others, who were perhaps influenced by lower property values compared with those in the south of England, took up residence. No longer were old buildings demolished to make way for ugly new ones; instead they were carefully restored and brought back into use. Tiny courtyards hidden behind Bridgegate and New Street were re-opened and mews-type cottages that had lain derelict and virtually forgotten for years were modernised without losing their character.

Gradually the momentum gathered and ambitious new shop and office developments were begun, but these were not flat-roofed, concrete structures; instead they were built to designs that would have pleased the architects of Retford's finest Georgian buildings. The journalist who described the town as moribund and tired after his visit in the 1970s returned in 1990 and wrote about the new vitality which he found evident. He liked the stylish new shops and the cobbled courtyards with Victorian lamps and noticed the rich variety of goods that are available in Chelsea-type shops and the feeling of renewed energy and pride in the town and its past.

Not all of the old traditions died in 1974. The town still appoints a Mayor and one of the highlights of the year is that of Mayor Making Day. It also still has a Lord High Steward, just as it has had since 1537, and civic processions continue to leave the Town Hall on their way to attend services in the Corporation church, where the Chairman of the District Council or the Town Mayor reads the lesson and the Councillors sit in the Corporation pews. Regrettably the processions are not, at present, led by a Sergeant at Mace bearing the huge ceremonial mace. That, along with the priceless collection of civic plate and other items, can be seen in the Bassetlaw Museum on Grove Street.

Retford is slowly being reborn and once again becoming a thriving and fashionable country market town that is proud of its past and confident about the future. In such an atmosphere the motto of the former Borough seems particularly appropriate. It can be seen in the ballroom of the Town Hall beneath the town's crest and reads —

'VETUSTAS DIGNITATEM GENERAT'

(Antiquity Generates Dignity)

Alley leading to Grove Street.

A forgotten back lane off Bridgegate.

KING EDWARD VI GRAMMAR SCHOOL
RETFORD

EX PULVERE PALMA

ORDER OF
COMMEMORATION SERVICE
AT 2.30 PM
ON FOUNDERS' DAY

WEDNESDAY, 8TH NOVEMBER, 1978

FOUR HUNDRED AND TWENTY-SEVENTH YEAR OF
KING EDWARD'S GRAMMAR SCHOOL

FOUR HUNDRED AND SIXTY-FIRST YEAR OF
THOMAS GUNTHORPE'S FOUNDATION

Founder's Day service at Retford Grammar School — the order sheet.

An 18th Century Dutch gabled building in Churchgate.

Trinity Hospital on Hospital Road.

Cannon Square.

War Memorial.

The Bassetlaw Museum, Grove Street, 2005.

The Masonic Hall, Carolgate Bridge, 2005.

Retford Railway Station 2005.

Willow Arches in Kings Park.

The Town Hall 2005.

Index

Select Bibliography

Barrymore Halpenny, B *Action Stations, Vol 2 Patrick Stevens 1981*
Briggs, A. A *Social History of England, Book Club Associates 1984*
Clark, Sir George *The Illustrated History of Britain, Octopus 1982*
Girouard, M. *The English Town, Guild Publishing, 1990*
Jackson, Allan *A History of Retford, Eaton Hall College 1971*
Piercy *History of Retford 1825*
Roffey, James *The Chesterfield Canal, Barracuda Books 1989*
Thomas, J.H *Town Government in the sixteenth Century, Allen 1933*
Victoria *History of Nottinghamshire*
Abelson, E.I. *Retford in Times Past, Retford and District Historical and Archeaological Society 1983*
Leleux, R.A. *A Regional History of the Railways of Great Britain Vol 9, The East Midlands David and Charles 1986*